PRESERVING TEXTILES

Indianapolis Museum of Art

PRESERVING TEXTILES

A Guide for the
Nonspecialist

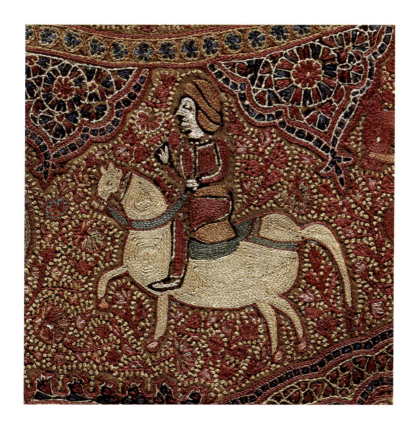

Harold F. Mailand
and Dorothy Stites Alig

© 1999 Indianapolis Museum of Art

All rights reserved
Printed in the United States of America

Published by the Indianapolis Museum of Art, 1200 West 38th Street, Indianapolis, IN 46208-4196

04 03 02 01 00 99   4 3 2 1

Library of Congress Cataloging-in-Publication Data

Mailand, Harold F.
    Preserving textiles : a guide for the nonspecialist / Harold F. Mailand and Dorothy Stites Alig.
        p.   cm.
    Includes bibliographical references and index.
    ISBN 0-936260-71-8 (paper)
    1. Textile fabrics—Conservation and restoration.   I. Title.
NK8804.5.M3424   1999
746'.028'8—dc21   99-16496

Drawings by Dorothy Stites Alig
Photography by Hadley Fruits
Edited by Jane Graham
Designed by Image Concepts

All works of art that are illustrated in this book are from the collection of the Indianapolis Museum of Art.

Cover and title page:
Detail from shawl, late 19th century, India, Punjab; wool, silk, 68 x 70 in.; Mary Black Fund, 1995.69.

CONTENTS

Foreword 7
Preface 9
Acknowledgments 11

Introduction 13
    Textile Conservation as a Profession
    Custodianship

The Environment 19
    Climate Control
    Lighting
    Mold
    Insects and Rodents

Treating Textiles 29
    Cleaning
        Surface Cleaning
        Wet Cleaning
        Spot Cleaning
        Dry Cleaning
    Humidification
    Stabilizing Damaged Areas

Archival Materials for Storage and Display 37

Storage 39
    Flat Storage
    Rolled Storage
    Costume Storage
    Framed or Mounted Textile Storage

Mounting and Exhibiting Textiles..................................47
    Velcro Fastener
    Fabric Sleeve
    Strainers and Solid Supports
    Passive Mounts
    Matting and Framing Textiles
    Pin Mounts
    Costume Mounts

Handling Guidelines 57
Plates 59
Glossary 71
Bibliography 75
Appendix A: Materials for Storage and Display 79
Appendix B: Supply Sources 80
Appendix C: Organizations 85
Index 89

FOREWORD

The Indianapolis Museum of Art was one of the first art institutions in the United States to collect textiles. The purchase in 1888 of a single embroidered item initiated the museum's 6,000-piece textile and costume collection, which today represents virtually all of the the world's traditions in fabrics. Textiles and costumes from the museum's collection are exhibited in appropriate cultural contexts in galleries throughout the institution. In addition, a special facility—the Dorit and Gerald Paul Gallery—has been created specifically for temporary exhibitions of textiles and costumes.

In recent years, the museum has demonstrated its continuing commitment to textile preservation with the installation of a new storage system for the entire textile and costume collection, incorporating the most current technology and archival storage methods. With a permanent textile exhibition space, state-of-the-art storage, a 1,000-square-foot textile conservation laboratory and a collection study room, the IMA is able to give its permanent collection the finest care while serving as a valuable resource for other institutions, groups and individuals.

In 1980, Harold F. Mailand, then textile conservator at the IMA, recognized the urgent need for accurate information about textile conservation for the nonspecialist. He addressed this need in a pioneering museum publication, *Considerations for the Care of Textiles and Costumes: A Handbook for the Non-Specialist*. The demand for this book has remained constant ever since, resulting in five reprintings in less than two decades.

In 1998, Dorothy Stites Alig, the museum's current textile conservator, invited Mr. Mailand, now a conservator in private practice, to collaborate on a new publication that would revisit the now classic handbook but substantially update its content and appearance. This book is the result of their collaboration.

Dorothy also deserves special recognition for contributing the illustrations and the appendices, which greatly enhance the guide's practical value.

The authors have been ably assisted in their endeavor by museum editor Jane Graham, museum photographer Tad Fruits, and the graphic design company Image Concepts. The enterprise has had the enthusiastic support of the museum's chief conservator, Martin Radecki. I congratulate all involved in the project and thank them on behalf of all the textile collectors and enthusiasts who will benefit from this new guide.

Bret Waller
Director, Indianapolis Museum of Art

PREFACE

Well-meaning collectors often ask textile conservators how to preserve artifacts in their collections while, at the same time, using or displaying them. Unfortunately, the answer must be: "the two goals of preservation and use are diametrically opposed." On a daily basis, museums face difficult decisions about making their collections accessible to visitors and scholars while preserving them for generations to come. A reasonable compromise can be found.

The authors of this guide hope that the information contained herein will assist textile collectors and custodians in making well-informed decisions that will lead to the preservation of these irreplaceable objects, as well as to the enjoyment of them. It is a practical guide for the nonspecialist, including employees of institutions that do not have professional conservation staffs, private collectors, and individuals responsible for family heirlooms. Please note that a glossary has been included to clarify some of the more specialized terminology; these terms are *italicized* in the text. For more in-depth information on many of the topics covered in this guide, please consult the bibliography and appendices in the back of the book.

The authors and the Indianapolis Museum of Art cannot be responsible for the interpretation of the contents of this guide.

ACKNOWLEDGMENTS

Many of my talented colleagues at the Indianapolis Museum of Art contributed to this book. Our director, Bret Waller, and Marty Radecki, chief conservator, recognized the need for an updated book on textile preservation and gave the project their solid support. Jane Graham, our editor, offered good counsel, encouragement, and, of course, good grammar. She deserves much credit. Tad Fruits contributed the wonderful photographs.

Colleagues in the Conservation Department lent their assistance and considerable knowledge—a special thanks to David Miller for reading an early draft. Jane Lee's contribution to the textile conservation lab is immeasurable and greatly appreciated. Many other IMA colleagues offered encouragement and expertise—a special thanks to Mike Bir, Deb Brennan, Niloo Paydar, Ruth Roberts, and Russ Wadler.

Nancy Meers of Image Concepts did a beautiful job with the design of the book and brought the perfect balance of creativity and diplomacy to the project.

David Mueller of Insects Limited was characteristically generous with his time and expertise. Alain Van Ryckeghem, Mary Ballard, Chris Paulocik, Jim Canary and David Galusha consulted on various details of the project.

Thanks to the residents of Casa Wapahana, especially Lee, Lucie and Jim, for their patience and encouragement.

Finally, I would like to thank my co-author, Harold Mailand, director of Textile Conservation Services and author of the first book published by the Indianapolis Museum of Art on the subject of textile preservation. When I invited Harold to collaborate on this new book, I had no idea how rewarding and enjoyable it would be to discuss, research, and articulate in writing the many facets of our shared profession.

Dorothy Stites Alig
Conservator of Textiles
Indianapolis Museum of Art
May 1999

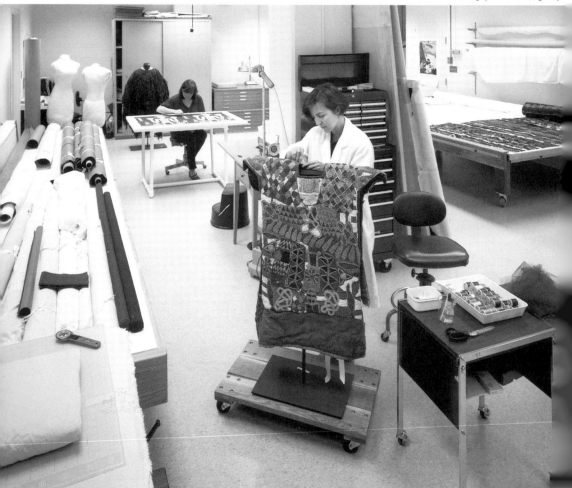

The textile conservation laboratory at the Indianapolis Museum of Art.

INTRODUCTION

The art of transforming fibers into wearing apparel, furnishing goods, and decorative or artistic objects has a history as long as civilization itself. Textiles give a richness to our surroundings, and when they are collected and studied, they can provide a more complete understanding of historic and artistic periods of the past.

Whether the textiles or costumes in a collection are handmade or machine-made, they may not be replaceable. These important objects therefore deserve the best possible housing and care. If they are not actively cared for, they will deteriorate, and those who care for them in the future may face the difficult decision of deaccessioning or providing costly conservation treatments. Damage often cannot be reversed even by a professional conservator. It is imperative, therefore, to be aware of the possible problems associated with the care of these vulnerable objects and the many avenues available to the owner or custodian to mitigate these problems. Good stewardship now will assure that future generations will be able to learn from and enjoy the rich textile and costume traditions from around the world.

Whether a private collector, gallery owner, museum or historical society staff member, often the most beneficial efforts of a custodian are simple things—good housekeeping, documentation, and familiarity with archival materials and environmental issues. Before undertaking any treatment, it is wise to ask: If I do this, can I undo it at a later date? If in doubt, it is best to do nothing and consult a professional conservator.

Textile Conservation as a Profession

In recent years, the conservation of cultural property has become an increasingly specialized profession, complete with national and regional professional organizations, advanced training opportunities, a refined code of ethics and guidelines for practice, and heightened public awareness.

While conservators are sometimes referred to as "art doctors," there are a number of approaches to preservation both in and outside of museums, and sometimes the terms for them are confused. **Restoration, conservation, preventative care** and **preservation,** may sound similar, but there are meaningful distinctions between them. These differences are revealed when we consider the objectives and training of their practitioners.

The primary objective of a **restorer** is to return a work of art to its assumed original appearance, sometimes at the expense of original material, sometimes by adding new material.

A **conservator** endeavors to stabilize a work of art and minimize further damage so that it can be fully enjoyed and interpreted. Conservators use their training in chemistry, studio art, and art history to examine works of art and to document the materials, methods of fabrication, and processes of deterioration involved. One of the guiding principles of conservation is reversibility: The material or treatment method used should be fully reversible, allowing the work of art to be treated again at a later date, should better materials or methods become available.

Conservators sometimes employ restoration techniques but avoid using materials that would be irreversible or that would compromise the artistic, physical, or historical integrity of the artifact.

Another important aspect of a conservator's job is **preventative care,** which involves improving the environment surrounding the work of art and ensuring that the materials in contact with it are of archival quality, thereby prolonging its life.

The objective of both conservation and preventative care is **preservation,** maintaining the physical integrity of cultural property and prolonging its existence. While conservators are important advocates for preservation, many other members of the museum staff, including registrars, curators, collection managers, art installers and packers, exhibit and lighting designers, and security staff, are also involved in this effort. Private collectors are important preservation advocates as well since most works of art, even those currently in museums, are privately owned for some period of time.

Many preservation measures can be implemented by well-informed museum staff and private collectors. It should be emphasized, however, that some of the more specialized procedures, particularly those involving cleaning and consolidation, are best left to a professional conservator.

INTRODUCTION

When in doubt, it is wise to consult a professional conservator. Begin by contacting a museum in your area, preferably one large enough to have some in-house conservation expertise, to inquire about qualified conservators. Another valuable source of information is the American Institute for Conservation of Historic and Artistic Works (AIC) and its Guide to Conservation Services, which provides names, specialties, membership levels, and locations of AIC members who can answer more specific questions and provide treatments (see Organizations).

When engaging the services of a professional conservator, expect him or her to examine the textile and provide a written report, proposal for treatment, and a cost estimate before work commences. Upon completion of the treatment, a professional conservator should supply the owner with a treatment report, which may include photographic documentation.

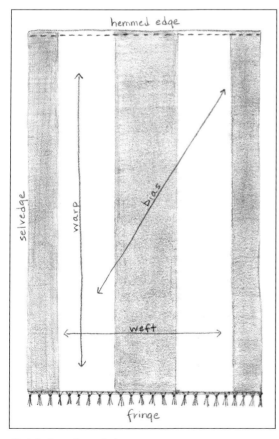

Fig. 1. Basic textile terminology

Custodianship

Whether you have textiles in your personal collection or work for a museum as a curator or registrar, you may find yourself acting as a custodian of a few or many examples of textiles of artistic or historical interest. Custodians have a responsibility to preserve the textiles in their care; depending on the scope and cultural significance of the pieces in their collections, they may also have a responsibility to examine and document them (fig. 1). The purpose of recording this information is twofold:

to provide a baseline record of the textile's condition and to provide documentation for insurance purposes.

Carefully examine each newly acquired textile (see Handling Guidelines on page 57). Looking at the materials and fabrication techniques is an important first step towards making informed decisions about its care, storage and display, and it is one of the pleasures of being the caretaker. It is also an opportunity to assess the condition of the work of art, noting structural as well as superficial weaknesses or damaged areas that might require conservation or special handling. It is worth noting the presence of materials that have *inherent vice,* inevitable deterioration due to weaknesses in the materials. Examples of inherent vice include black and dark brown fabrics that deteriorate due to an iron *mordant* used in the dyeing process (fig. 2; see also image on title page) and *"weighted silks"* that shatter because of metallic salts added during manufacture (fig. 3).

Fig. 2. Fiber loss (white areas) in an Indonesian textile resulting from a mordant in the dye (inherent vice). See also Plate 10 and image on title page.

Following assessment, the new acquisition should be photographed and vacuumed, if its condition permits. If there are any signs of insect activity, past or present, the textile should be isolated for several weeks before being integrated into the main storage area. Wrap the textile in polyethylene plastic sheeting and seal it closed with tape. After two or three weeks, examine the package for any evidence of insect activity (see Insects and Rodents).

INTRODUCTION

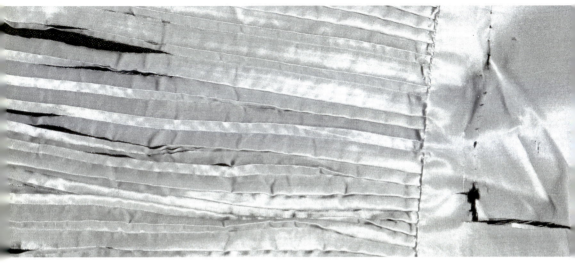

Fig. 3. Shattered silk

All observations and treatment measures should be summarized in writing and dated so that it will be possible to monitor changes in the appearance and condition of the textile over a period of years (fig. 4). These notes, as well as any photographic documentation, diagrams, components of the textile that have become detached, and old labels or identification tags are important documentation and should be kept in a file labeled with the textile's accession or identification number. ■

```
Identification #:
Description:
Dimensions:
Materials:
Condition:

History:


Examined by:                    Date:
```

Fig. 4. Identification card, for recording information about a textile

How to Label a Textile

If a collection consists of more than a few textiles, each piece should be identified with a number that corresponds to a numeric record file that contains more specific information on the textile. An archival cloth label can be made by printing the number on a small piece of cotton twill tape that has been coated with an acrylic fixative, such as Krylon (see Supply Sources). After writing or typing the number in indelible ink, spray the label with another layer of Krylon to prevent smudging. When it is dry, the label can be stitched into a corner of the textile on the back (fig. 5). If this method is not appropriate for the piece, a small acid-free drop tag can be attached to the textile with cotton thread. When textiles are labeled in a consistent place and manner, they can be identified easily and unnecessary handling can be avoided. Never use staples, pins or adhesives, which may rust or become discolored and may be difficult to remove.

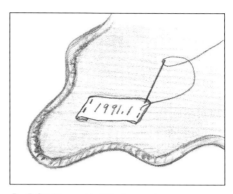

Fig. 5. Stitching an identification number on the back of a textile

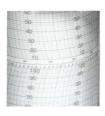

THE ENVIRONMENT

Controlling the environment surrounding a textile is the single most important means of ensuring its preservation. Establishing good preventative maintenance practices is more cost-efficient in the long run and prevents damage to the works of art that may be untreatable or expensive to treat.

Climate Control

Although textiles and costumes have been preserved in extreme environmental conditions, ranging from the desert to frozen terrain, it is advisable to preserve a collection under more controlled conditions. The natural fibers (cotton, linen, wool and silk) that are found in most textile collections expand and contract according to the temperature and moisture content of the surrounding air. Severe and rapid changes in humidity especially but also in temperature cause swelling and shrinking of the fibers. As a result, the fibers may lose their natural properties of resiliency, elasticity and *tensile strength*. High humidity also encourages mold growth and insects.

It is recommended that textiles be placed in a controlled environment with a temperature of 70°F + or - 5°F (21°C + or - 3°C) and a *relative humidity* level of 50% + or - 5%. The objective is to provide an environment that can be stabilized within these temperature and humidity ranges and to avoid severe and/or rapid changes outside these ranges. Place *hygrometers* and thermometers throughout the exhibition and storage areas for easy reference, and record the data on a regular basis (fig. 6). This data will be particularly helpful if it is necessary to work with architectural conservators; engineers; heating, ventilation, and air conditioning (HVAC) consultants, or other specialists to design a climate-control system. A well-designed system will accommodate the needs of the collection without causing stress (in the form of excessive condensation) on the building. This is an especially important consideration for historic structures.

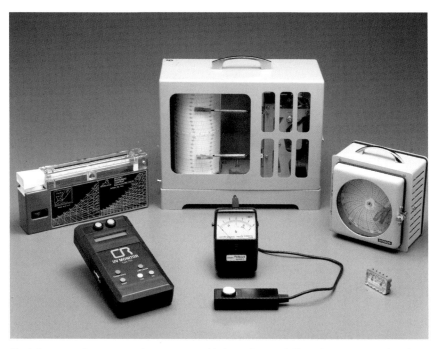

Fig. 6. Equipment for monitoring the environment: (clockwise from top left) psychrometer, two styles of recording hygrothermographs, temperature and relative humidity gauge, light meter, and UV light meter

Textiles should not be housed in basements or attics where humidity and temperatures can reach extremes. It is recommended that all textiles be stored in a centrally located storage space that is heated and air-conditioned. Portable fans, heaters, humidifiers, dehumidifiers, and air-conditioning units can be used to maintain stable conditions throughout the year.

Good air circulation is another requirement. Because most residential and commercial buildings have forced-air systems, the air must be filtered to minimize the particulate matter that may be present in the system. The air in exhibition cases and enclosed storage cabinets can be filtered by placing commercial filter products or common materials such as Pellon or flannel over pre-cut holes near the top of the unit. Check the filters on a regular basis, and change them when they are dirty.

THE ENVIRONMENT

Lighting

The effect of light on textiles needs to be seriously considered. Light is a form of energy existing in a broad spectrum of both visible and invisible waves. Both visible and ultraviolet light can cause fading and the internal breakdown of textile fibers (fig. 7). Depending on the dye type and fiber, this damage can occur in a very short time and sometimes is not detected until after cleaning, when slits or holes occur.

Damage caused by light is cumulative and irreversible; it is accelerated in the presence of high temperatures, high humidity, and atmospheric pollutants.

To protect textiles, avoid lighting that is too intense, produces excessive heat, or has a high degree of ultraviolet radiation. Sunlight is the major source of ultraviolet light and should be avoided in storage and exhibition areas if at all possible. If windows cannot be eliminated, they should be treated with an ultraviolet-filtering film as well as black-out blinds. Ultraviolet-filtering acrylic sheeting can be used in exhibition cases and frames for additional protection.

Fluorescent lights also generate an unacceptable amount of ultraviolet radiation. Fluorescent tubes, whether in a work area or in a display case, must always be covered with ultraviolet-filtering sheaths. These filters, which slide over each tube, lose their effectiveness after a few years and should be replaced. On the positive side, fluorescent light produces less heat than incandescent light, an important consideration when lighting enclosed cases, where too much heat may be a serious problem.

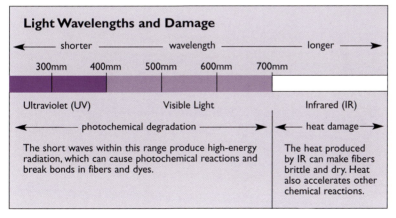

Fig. 7. The effect of light on textiles

Incandescent lights have been the staple of museum lighting systems for years. This type of lighting has a negligible ultraviolet output, but a high infrared output. The major concern with incandescent lights is the heat that they generate. Incandescent lights are used at a distance from the exhibited object rather than in an enclosed case, where they would raise the case temperature, lower the relative humidity, and dry out the textile.

New government regulations that place restrictions on the manufacture of certain commonly used incandescent bulbs are forcing museums to rethink their lighting options. Many institutions will rely more on halogen bulbs, which unfortunately emit significant amounts of ultraviolet radiation. Ultraviolet filters for each bulb will be necessary, but costly.

Calculating Light Exposure

Any amount of light exposure will cause some degree of fading and deterioration. How can we reach a compromise between visibility and preservation? The law of reciprocity applies to display lighting. The degree of damage is based on a combination of two factors: intensity and duration of exposure. If either of these factors is increased, the other can be decreased proportionately and the amount of damage will remain constant. For example, a textile on display at 6 footcandles for 2 months will receive the same amount of light damage as a textile displayed at 3 footcandles for 4 months.

Another lighting system that is gaining popularity in museums is fiber-optic lighting. This system employs a light source, usually halogen, that can be directed to the subject through one or a series of glass or acrylic rods. This technology is a promising alternative to conventional lighting since the ultraviolet waves can be filtered at the source, it does not generate heat, and it is superior in situations where very precise control of the level of illumination is required.

The decision about the appropriate level of illumination is always a difficult one. Any amount of light will cause damage, so the objective is to use the minimal intensity that will allow the textile to be seen clearly by the museum's visitors, even those with imperfect vision. Museums have traditionally found that 5-7 *footcandles* (50-70 *lux*) satisfy these requirements for very light-sensitive materials, such as textiles. A light meter is a worthwhile investment for any institution or individual with a textile collection.

Even at these low levels of illumination, all light-sensitive materials should be taken off display according to a rotation schedule that allows the textiles to remain in storage, away from all illumination, for as long as possible. This rotation schedule should take into account the mechanical and structural stress associated with moving, rolling, folding, and rehousing the object, especially a large textile, such as a tapestry or flag, and very fragile textiles or costumes. In some cases, longer display periods with lower light levels might be worth considering.

Light damage can also occur in work and storage areas. Turn appropriately filtered lights on or open window coverings only when necessary for viewing or working. Textiles on work tables that are not being examined or treated should be covered with a layer of acid-free tissue or muslin.

Creative solutions to the lighting dilemma should be considered whenever possible. Investigate visitor-activated lighting, transition lighting between galleries that allows the eyes to adjust, black-out materials, or perhaps even flashlights available upon request.

Mold

Molds, including mildew, are microscopic spores of fungi. Mold spores are always present in the air and can grow on any organic material, including fibers, provided the conditions are favorable. One of these conditions is a relative humidity over 65%. Prolonged exposure to mold will cause staining and structural breakdown of the fibers.

To prevent the growth of mold, maintain a relative humidity level below 60% and good air circulation. Do not store textiles in a basement or in areas where water leakage is possible. If the humidity levels cannot be controlled, at least provide good air circulation. A textile in humid conditions in an airtight frame or in direct contact with glass, acrylic sheeting, or plastic sheeting is a good candidate for mold growth and damage.

Mold spores will be killed or discouraged if the textile is placed in a room with circulating dry air, or taken outdoors on a sunny day when the relative humidity is low. Controlled exposure to the ultraviolet component present in sunlight is an effective means of killing the mold spores, but keep exposure time under an hour, especially for colored objects. Mold growth can also be killed by using a low setting on a portable hair dryer held at least 12 inches away from the piece. Remove the desiccated spores by vacuuming the entire piece. If mold occurs on washable objects, brushing or vacuuming followed by *wet cleaning* may be warranted. Mold spores are very obstinate and may become active again if the conditions are favorable. It may be necessary to use the strongest treatment that the textile can withstand to minimize the risk of regrowth.

When handling a textile that has mold growth, keep in mind that some types of mold pose health problems. Appropriate safety equipment such as a respirator, gloves, and a vacuum with a *HEPA* (high efficiency particulate air) *filter* or *water-trap* system may be required. It is also important to take precautions to prevent the transfer of spores from one textile to another.

Insects and Rodents

Certain insects and rodents can cause considerable damage to a textile collection. Rather than responding with panic to an existing pest problem, try to prevent such a crisis by developing an integrated pest management (IPM) plan. A successful IPM plan discourages pests by controlling the environment, eliminating food sources and access points, and monitoring susceptible areas. The success of the plan will depend on the custodian's familiarity with the varieties of destructive pests and their habits and preferences.

Begin with good housekeeping since a clean environment offers fewer sources of food and makes it easier to detect new signs of insect activity. Vacuum storage areas frequently and promptly discard vacuum cleaner bags. Remember, anything made of protein—hair, lint, dead insects—even the contents of the vacuum cleaner bag, is a potential food source for carpet beetles and clothes moths.

The collection, as well as storage units and materials, should be regularly inspected for signs of insect activity. Monitor the storage area by placing "sticky traps" along baseboards, near doors, on window sills, and adjacent to other points of intrusion. It may be necessary to try several locations before ruling out the presence of insects. *Pheromone traps*, which use chemical lures to attract the male insect, are another effective monitoring device. Inspect the traps and replace them regularly so it will be possible to distinguish newly collected specimens. Inspect the building for abandoned bird and wasp nests located near the storage areas. These nests can become feeding and breeding grounds for carpet beetles.

Clothes moths *(Tineola bisselliella)* and carpet beetles *(Anthrenus verbasci)* are attracted to textiles with protein content (silk, wool, fur and feathers), especially if these materials are soiled with food or dirt (fig. 8). If possible, segregate the above materials and monitor them more frequently. During the larval stage, when they feed and cause damage, these pests prefer dark, quiet areas. Vacuuming or brushing the textiles will disrupt the insects and may kill fragile eggs but are not totally effective. Aromatic deterrents such as cedar wood and herbal combinations may repel some pests, but will not kill them. Paradichlorobenzene, the active ingredient in mothballs, is considered harmful to humans and can no longer be recommended.

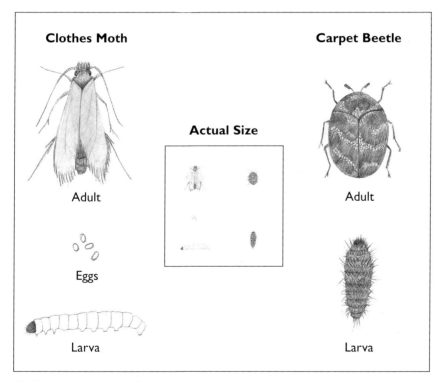

Fig. 8. Insects that damage textiles

How to Freeze a Textile

Most textiles will need to be folded or rolled to fit into the freezer. Wrap the artifact in a layer of muslin or acid-free tissue (to absorb any condensation), and then seal it in an envelope of polyethylene plastic sheeting. Eliminate as much excess air as possible from the envelope and carefully tape it closed. A sticky tape such as duct tape is recommended since some tapes might not stick at freezing temperatures. The bag must be completely sealed so outside air cannot penetrate, increasing the risk of condensation.

The package must be brought from room temperature to a frozen state quickly (within a few hours), as insects can adapt to a gradual change. While some insects will be killed after two or three days, it is recommended that the textile be left in the freezer (at -4°F) for a week to ensure that all species and stages of the insects are killed (Thomas J. K. Strang, "A Review of Published Temperatures for the Control of Pest Insects in Museums," Collection Forum 8, no. 2[1992]: 41-67).

When the package is removed from the freezer, allow it to slowly return to room temperature. Depending on the density of the textile, this will take a day or two. Some condensation will form on the outside of the plastic, but this is not cause for concern. Warning: Do not open the package prematurely as this may result in the formation of condensation on the textile. When the textile has returned to room temperature, take it out of the plastic, examine it carefully, and brush or vacuum away any insect debris.

It is relatively rare to find a live adult clothes moth or carpet beetle. Often the first sign of a beetle problem is a cast skin, or casing. With clothes moths, the first indication is often a silky cocoon or frass (excreta) that bears the color of the digested fiber. Another indication of insect activity is damage to the textile, usually in the form of cleanly excised holes in the fabric or tunnel-like excavations in a thicker fabric or pile (see Plate 1). Since it is sometimes difficult to discern whether the insect activity is past or current, it is wise to actively monitor the situation.

Silverfish feed on materials containing starch, often present in natural glues and paste (wheat, rice, skin) and sizings, and in pursuit of these, they can cause structural damage to textile fibers. Segregate and monitor textiles that have paper components or that are heavily starched. Keeping storage areas clean and within the recommended temperature and humidity levels will discourage silverfish. Monitor with sticky traps placed near pipes, drains and other damp places.

Mice and rats can also cause damage to textiles through their food scavenging and nesting patterns. Snap traps and sticky traps or a professional pest manager can prove effective in controlling these pests. Do not use poison bait as this may cause the rodent to die between walls and thus become a host for carpet beetles. Locate and seal off possible points of entry.

Monitor the spider population around storage areas; spiders do not eat textiles, but they do eat other insects. A thriving spider population may indicate the presence of other undesirable insects in the vicinity. Until recently, fumigation was the first line of defense when an insect problem was identified in a museum. Current concerns about the health risks of these chemicals and the potential for damage to works of art have led to the development of alternative methods of pest control. These include freezing, oxygen deprivation and CO_2 exposure.

Of these methods, freezing is the simplest and most practical. In order to kill all stages of the insect (egg, larva, and adult), the textile should be exposed to temperatures of - 4°F (- 20°C) for seven days. Most textile fibers respond well to freezing, but brittle components such as plastics and adhesives must be handled with extreme caution as they are especially vulnerable to damage during the freezing and thawing process. Very brittle materials and non-absorbent materials (glass, metal, ceramic) should not be frozen.

If infestations persist, consult a professional pest manager, preferably someone who has experience working with museums or historic homes. Inquire about pest management strategies such as the use of pheromone traps to collect and identify specific insects. Never spray any chemical directly onto the textile or any other work of art. ■

TREATING TEXTILES

Cleaning

One of the first and most compelling instincts of most textile custodians is to clean. Whether this stems from the fact that the textile is genuinely disfigured by dirt or stains or from well-intentioned but overzealous housekeeping tendencies, this step must be carefully considered. Although most of the treatment procedures used by textile conservators are reversible, some cleaning methods are not. If dyes bleed or the texture is altered, the damage is often permanent. Cleaning is a means of neutralizing the *pH* of the textile and removing stains or particulate matter that may weaken the fiber. Often the appearance of the textile will not improve dramatically, especially if the stains have been there for some time. Cleaning methods include surface cleaning, wet cleaning, and dry cleaning.

Surface Cleaning

Surface cleaning involves the mechanical removal of lint, grit, and other particulate matter from the surface of the textile. Brushing with a very soft brush from an art supply store is the gentlest treatment and is appropriate for very delicate textiles. For sturdier items in the collection, vacuuming is the more effective and readily available cleaning method. All but the most fragile textiles can withstand vacuuming if the special equipment and techniques discussed below are used. With most types of vacuum cleaners, the amount of suction can be controlled by opening the vents, using a low-powered setting, or plugging the vacuum into a variable output transformer. If mold spores or potential irritants are present, it may be necessary to use a vacuum with a HEPA filter or water-trap system.

The choice of attachment will depend on the size and condition of the textile; both the soft brush and the smooth-edged attachments are useful. Micro-attachments that adapt to most vacuum cleaners are well suited to delicate jobs and are reasonably priced(see Supply Sources). Clean attachments and change filter bags between uses.

Fig. 9. Vacuuming through a screen

It may be helpful to place a square of Fiberglas screening, edged in twill tape, on top of fragile textiles during vacuuming. This screening protects the textile from strong suction, abrasion, and fiber loss (fig. 9).

In preparation for vacuuming, lay the textile flat on a clean, smooth surface. Vacuum carefully, moving in a regular pattern to help track the areas already covered. If there is a nap or pile, vacuum in the direction of the pile. Clean the support surface before turning over the textile to vacuum the back. If the textile must be rolled as it is vacuumed, be sure to clean the back as well, to avoid transferring dirt from that side to the clean one.

Frequency of vacuuming will depend on the condition of the textile and how it is used or exhibited. Textiles that are displayed horizontally or at an angle will require more frequent maintenance. It is important to inspect and vacuum the underside of rugs to remove grit and to deter carpet beetles and moths. Textiles that have brittle fibers or delicate surface features may not be able to tolerate frequent vacuuming, if at all.

Wet Cleaning

Wet cleaning is the process whereby the textile is cleaned in water, often with a detergent solution. The goal in wet cleaning is to neutralize the pH of the object, soften and remove water-soluble stains, and flush out particulate matter. Many stains, especially older stains, may not respond to wet cleaning. Improved design clarity and color are sometimes an added benefit.

The use of water and chemical solutions to clean textiles of historical or artistic significance must be carefully considered. Wet cleaning is an irreversible process and cannot be stopped once it is started. During the cleaning

TREATING TEXTILES

and drying process, dyes, finishes, and important biological, historical or aesthetic information may be removed or altered. Conservators are well aware of the risks associated with wet cleaning; all but the most routine wet cleaning is best left to a professional.

Before cleaning, it is essential to determine if the textile's dyes are colorfast. Test an inconspicuous colored area with a drop of water at wash temperature, let it soak in, and press with a white cloth or absorbent paper. If no color is transferred, apply a drop of the detergent solution that will be used to clean the textile and check again to see if any color transfers onto the white blotting material. Check all colored areas of the textile in this fashion. If any of the colors bleed, stop; the wet cleaning process should not be employed by a nonspecialist.

If a textile has any of the features below, it should not be wet-cleaned by a nonspecialist:
- *Delicate, brittle or powdering fibers*
- *Fugitive dyes*
- *Original finishes or surface effects (moire, glazing)*
- *Silk embroidery floss*
- *High-twist yarns*
- *Painted surfaces or soluble adhesives*
- *Composite or multilayered materials*
- *Paper elements, including gilded paper*
- *Velvet*
- *Leather or feathers*
- *Sequins*
- *Unknown components*

If the textile is colorfast, decide whether it will be immersed in water alone or in a detergent solution. Soaps should be avoided because they react with the ions in hard water and form precipitates, which can be deposited on the textile. Laundry detergents and special cleaning products contain additives such as whiteners, optical brighteners, dyes, and fragrances, which may not rinse out entirely and may have unpredictable long-term effects on old textiles. Textile conservators often use an anionic detergent such as Orvus WA Paste (sodium lauryl sulfate)(see Supply Sources). If this is not available, use a very mild dishwashing detergent that is free of the additives mentioned above. Generally speaking, one tablespoon of detergent for each gallon of water will make an efficient cleaning solution. Higher concentrations of detergent may complicate thorough rinsing.

For cleaning, it is best to use the purest water available, preferably *distilled* or *deionized water*. If water of this quality is not available in large quantities, at least try to provide the purest water possible for the final rinse. A portable or in-line water filter system can deliver an improved quality

> *Valuable textiles should never be placed in automatic washers and dryers. The agitation and space constrictions of a washer place too much strain on old fibers and may cause abrasion and shredding. In addition, the textile and wash solution are more difficult to see and cannot be monitored for problems, such as fugitive dyes, that may develop unexpectedly. Likewise, the heat and tumbling of a dryer accelerate the breakdown of fibers.*

of tap water but it may still contain impurities. Water that is very hard or that contains metal ions such as iron and other impurities should not be used, as the residue left behind can stain and, over time, cause the deterioration of textile fibers.

The bath chamber can be made of any *inert* material; stainless steel, porcelain and plastic photographic trays are suitable for small textiles. Bath tubs, sinks, and wooden frames can be made inert with a lining of polyethylene plastic sheeting. The wet-cleaning chamber should be large enough to accommodate the entire textile as flat as possible.

Vacuum stable textiles to remove dust and grit prior to cleaning to minimize the abrasive action of these particulates in the water bath. Place the textile on a length of white polyester Reemay, a cotton sheet, or if the textile is very sturdy, a layer of Fiberglas screening that is larger than the piece. This support material serves as a flexible cradle, allowing the entire textile to be moved or suspended with minimum stress (fig. 10).

Fig. 10. Using a support material while washing a textile

When the textile is prepared for wet cleaning, gently submerge it in the detergent solution at 80°F to 90°F. Soaking time will vary from a few minutes up to 15 minutes. If the textile is badly soiled but strong, the detergent bath can be repeated for more thorough cleaning. Keep agitation to a minimum, as most fibers are weakest while wet. If the textile is heavily soiled but strong, use a clean cellulose sponge to gently move the detergent solution through the textile by pressing down evenly on the sponge with an open hand, and then releasing the pressure. Rinse at least four times or until no trace of detergent remains. The final rinse should be nearly neutral, or 7.0 on the pH scale; however, the pH of the water used for washing will also affect all subsequent readings. This can be checked with pH paper strips or a pH meter before, during, and after the wash bath.

When the rinsing is complete, cover the textile with clean white cotton toweling, mattress padding, sheeting, or muslin and press gently to remove excess water. It may be necessary to repeat this moisture extraction process several times, so plan on having lots of the absorbent materials on hand. To promote efficient drying, remove as much water as possible at this stage. Dry the textile on a clean, flat surface or on an elevated screen in a well-ventilated area. Fans will increase air circulation and accelerate drying.

The textile can be gently blocked while it is still damp. Many textiles are distorted because of use or the method of construction; it is unlikely that this can be corrected by blocking. Avoid pulling excessively on the fibers, which are especially vulnerable when damp. Pinning often creates more distortion as many textiles shrink slightly as they dry. Drying flat textiles on a slick surface, such as glass, may result in a crisp, pressed appearance.

During drying, a thin fabric, such as cheesecloth or muslin, may be placed on top of and in close contact with a thick or multilayered textile such as a quilt. This added layer draws impurities such as degraded cellulose away from the surface of the textile through capillary action.

Historical textiles should not be pressed with a hot iron since the amount of heat and pressure required to accomplish the desired results may damage delicate fibers or cause scorch marks or undesirable surface effects. The heat of the iron may also set stains, making them more difficult to remove at a later date.

Remember, the prime reason for wet cleaning is to return the textile to a clean, neutral and stable condition. Often, there will be no visible change in appearance. The cleaning method outlined above is recommended only for a colorfast textile in good condition.

Spot Cleaning

If a stained textile cannot be immersed because of bleeding dyes, it is often tempting to consider spot cleaning as an alternative. While this technique may be successfully employed by a professional conservator or dry cleaner with the aid of specialized spotting or vacuum extraction systems, it is often disastrous in less experienced hands. When a drop of cleaning solution is applied to a stain, that solvent and solubilized components of the stain will spread, forming a larger circle that will leave dark edges, or tide lines, after it dries (see Plate 1).

Another undesirable effect occurs when the textile is discolored overall (which is often the case, though it may not be obvious). In this situation, the cleaning solution works so well that it leaves a conspicuously lighter, cleaner spot in the midst of an otherwise evenly discolored field. For all of the above reasons, the temptation to spot clean a historical textile should be resisted.

Dry Cleaning

Dry cleaning, or *solvent* cleaning, is an effective means of removing oil-based stains, but is not as satisfactory in removing water-based stains. Professional dry cleaners use a "closed" or "dry to dry" system: The fabric is placed in a dry cleaning machine to which solvent is automatically added; the soiled fabrics are then tumbled in the solvent, the solvent is extracted, and finally the fabrics are tumble-dried with heat. This procedure involves a high degree of mechanical action and heat, which can place too much strain on old fibers and may cause irreversible damage, such as abrasion and splitting.

A few specialists provide an alternative "tray" cleaning system, in which a rigid mesh tray is inserted into the drum. The tray supports the fabric, which is wrapped in batting, allowing it to remain stationary during the solvent cleaning, extraction and drying process.

In general, only contemporary and/or very sturdy textiles are candidates for dry cleaning, and only if they exhibit oil or grease stains. Insist that fresh solvent be used and that the dyes be tested. Textiles should be cleaned with like-colored items, since dirty solvent or fugitive dyes in the same load can discolor white or light-colored fabrics. For further protection, delicate

TREATING TEXTILES

fabrics can be placed in a mesh bag or custom-made enclosure before cleaning.

If possible, consult with a dry cleaner who is associated with the International Fabricare Institute (IFI)(see Organizations) and who has passed the Professional Dry Cleaning Certificate exam.

> *Do not store textiles or clothing items in dry-cleaning bags or "department store" tissue paper, as these materials are unlikely to be archival.*

Humidification

Controlled steaming and ultrasonic humidification can aid in shaping and blocking fiber objects and are very helpful in relaxing wrinkles and creases. The textile should be as clean as possible and vacuumed before humidification. Otherwise, stains and surface dirt may become permanently bonded to the fibers after humidification. Avoid placing the steamer head directly on the textile; intense heat and condensation from such close contact can damage the textile. High-twist fabrics such as chiffon and crepe should not be humidified as the twist will relax and lose the intended shape. Textiles with fugitive dyes or finishes are also poor candidates for humidification. It is always wise to test an inconspicuous area first.

Stabilizing Damaged Areas

Textiles and costumes often have fiber damage or loss in the form of holes, tears, abrasions or frayed edges. Factors such as age, fiber content, manufacturing processes, and patterns of use and care may accelerate the rate of damage.

While unsightly, these signs of wear and tear must be carefully considered and, in some cases, preserved, since they may provide insight into the unique history or "story line" of the textile or costume. Erasing or obscuring this information may have an adverse effect on the textile's historical or monetary value.

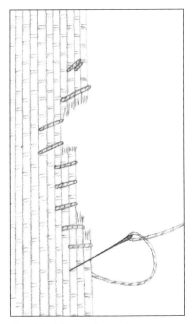

Fig. 11. Stabilizing a damaged edge with a whip stitch

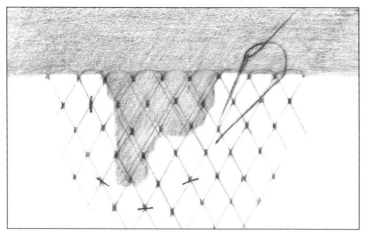

Fig. 12. Using nylon net to stabilize an area of loss

Stabilization of fiber loss is an aspect of treatment that falls into the category of conservation rather than preservation and therefore should be left to a professional conservator. Appropriate stabilization of areas of weakness or fiber loss is a complex undertaking. It requires a familiarity with a wide range of materials, their chemical and physical characteristics, and their long-term aging properties. It requires knowledge of specialized sewing, weaving, and adhesive techniques and the ability to skillfully execute them. Finally, a successful repair will reflect the conservator's awareness of color and design considerations and knowledge of textile history and aesthetics. It is beyond the scope of this guide to address all of these considerations.

When fiber loss or damage is a concern, minimal intervention is the best course of action for the nonspecialist. Prevent further damage by removing the textile from the threatening environment as soon as possible. Simple first aid may be warranted, such as a whip stitch to stabilize a raveling edge or tear (fig. 11). Nylon net may be placed over and behind a vulnerable hole or edge and stitched loosely into place with a running stitch (fig. 12). These measures will protect a damaged area until a carefully considered long-term solution can be devised, preferably based on consultations with a professional textile conservator. ■

ARCHIVAL MATERIALS FOR STORAGE AND DISPLAY

In recent years, much new information about the importance of using high-quality storage and display materials has come to light. New *archival materials*—those that are chemically inert and physically stable—have been developed and put to use. Many other materials commonly found in museum storage areas and display cases have been banished. Paper, cardboard, wood and wood products, even certain paints and coatings are inappropriate for contact with works of art because they emit volatile acids or other damaging chemicals, a process sometimes referred to as *offgassing*. Adhesives, such as urea-formaldehyde, used to bind the wood particles together in many inexpensive wood products, including plywood and particle board, may also emit acids that are damaging to fibers and metallic elements.

Consideration should be given to any material that comes into contact, especially prolonged contact, with a textile or costume. It is often a challenge for the textile custodian to distinguish an archival material from one that is not archival since the two may look identical. Plastic sheeting is one example since archival-quality polyethylene sheeting is difficult to distinguish from one containing polyvinyl chloride. The latter may release hydrochloric acid under certain conditions and should not be used. Other materials, such as tissue paper and foam products, pose similar difficulties. Department store tissue paper and the blue tissue paper supplied by dry cleaners in years past are not archival.

Before using a new material, or even a new batch of a familiar material, conservators often perform tests to detect the presence of harmful components. It may be impractical for a small museum or private collector to perform such tests. One easy way to check the pH of a paper product (never the artifact itself!) is with a pH pen, which turns the paper a color that indicates its acidity or alkalinity. The best way to ensure archival

Archival Materials and pH

Whenever possible, consider the fiber content of the textile and select archival materials accordingly (fig. 13). Protein fibers such as silk and wool require unbuffered acid-free materials, as they are more stable in neutral conditions. Cellulose materials, such as cotton and linen, will benefit from the alkaline environment provided by buffered archival products. If a textile contains both cellulose and protein fibers, or unknown fibers, use unbuffered acid-free materials.

Another alternative worth considering is archival papers and boxes that act as a molecular sieve, trapping acids and other atmospheric pollutants in the exterior layer while providing a buffered surface on the box's interior (see Supply Sources).

Archival materials will themselves become more acidic after prolonged contact with an acidic artifact. Therefore, archival papers that become discolored or stained should be replaced. Likewise, muslin used for storage should be laundered periodically.

quality is to purchase materials of a known composition from a reputable supplier. A list of recommended materials and suppliers can be found at the end of this book.

Storage and display furniture must also be made of materials that are inert or can be made inert. Corrosion and condensation can be a problem with some types of metal shelving, especially in humid conditions. To be safe, storage units other than powder-coated steel and aluminum should be treated with an inert sealant or physical barrier material such as plastic sheeting, Marvaseal, Mylar, heavy-weight acid-free paper or acid-free foam board. ■

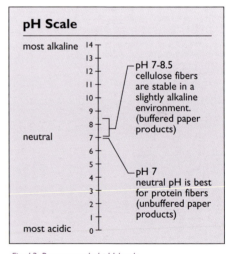

Fig. 13. Recommended pH levels

STORAGE

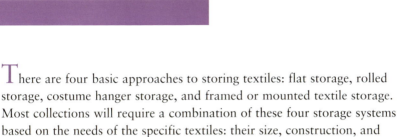

There are four basic approaches to storing textiles: flat storage, rolled storage, costume hanger storage, and framed or mounted textile storage. Most collections will require a combination of these four storage systems based on the needs of the specific textiles: their size, construction, and condition. Budget considerations and the availability of storage space and cabinetry will be important considerations as well.

Fig. 14. Rolled textiles suspended on supports, with drawers for flat storage in background

Flat Storage

Flat storage allows the textile to rest in a horizontal position, permitting the fibers to relax and the textile to maintain its natural tension. The housing unit might be an acid-free box, shelf, or drawer that is large enough to accommodate the entire textile or costume laid flat. Ideally, the textile should be stored with no folding; however if the housing does not allow this, then the textile should be folded, with acid-free tissue paper crumpled into the shape of a roll and placed inside the fold to prevent sharp creases from forming (fig. 15).

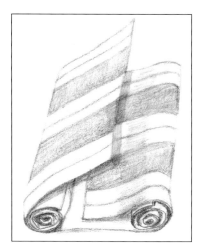

Fig. 15. Using acid-free tissue rolls to pad a folded textile

As fibers age, they become less flexible and may eventually split where consistent creases and pressure are placed. Therefore, if possible, avoid making the folds along well-established creases.

If the textile contains metallic threads or elements, place a sheet of acid-free tissue paper between the layers to protect adjacent areas of the textile or other textiles from coming into contact with sharp elements or corrosion products.

When costumes are folded, creases or folds should be padded with rolls of acid-free paper. If the costume is stored in an archival costume box, a layer of washed muslin, Tyvek or acid-free paper can be placed under the costume to allow it to be easily removed from the box (fig. 16).

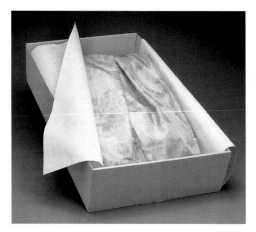

Fig. 16. An archival costume box with a Tyvek support under the costume

Rolled Storage

Rolled storage is well suited to pieces that are stable and strong but too large or heavy to be housed flat in shelves or drawers. The main support for the textile is a cardboard tube two to six inches in diameter, depending on the condition, size, and weight of the textile (a larger diameter tube places less stress on the textile). Acid-free tubes can be purchased, or non-archival cardboard tubes can be modified by covering them with several layers of Mylar, polyethylene plastic sheeting, Tyvek, or heavy-weight acid-free paper to prevent the acids in the cardboard from leaching through to the textile.

Before rolling, lay the textile flat and face down on a table or other clean surface large enough to accommodate the entire piece. Smooth out bulges and fold marks. Align the top and bottom ends, as well as *selvedges*, by using the edge of the table as a straight edge. In most cases, the tube should be positioned perpendicular to the *warp* threads, so the cut edge or *fringe* runs parallel to the tube. The back of the textile should be against the tube so that the face is exposed when the textile is rolled. *Pile* fabrics, such as velvets and rugs, should be rolled as above in the direction of the pile (fig. 17). Two or more people may be needed to roll textiles that are wider than three feet. Try to keep the edges coiling as uniformly as possible with consistent tension, preventing slack areas that may form sharp creases as they are transferred onto the roll.

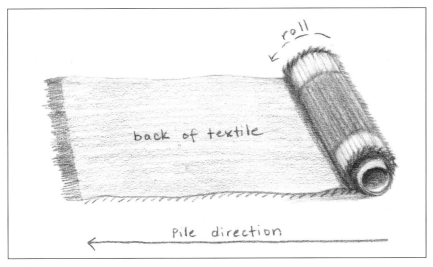

Fig. 17. Rolling a textile with a pile surface

When rolling textiles with fringe, it may be helpful to make a fringe folder, using acid-free tissue paper, the width of the textile. The end of the textile, including any fringe, is placed inside this folder to facilitate even rolling (fig. 18).

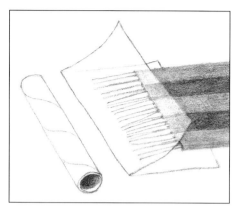

Fig. 18. A fringe folder

Special attention must be given to multilayered textiles, such as coverlets, quilts, and lined rugs and tapestries. When such objects are rolled, the tension on the face may be different from the tension on the back, creating strain on one side and wrinkles and creases on the other. Such textiles may benefit from a tube with a larger diameter or from another storage method if the problem is severe. In extreme cases, full linings may have to be loosened or removed.

Cover the rolled textile with Tyvek, clean cotton sheeting, or heavy-weight acid–free tissue and secure with twill tape ties at regular intervals. Attach a drop tag to the outside of each covered textile to identify it.

Rolled textiles can be housed in several ways. If possible, the roll should be suspended so that no part is resting against a flat surface. This can be accomplished with a length of electrical conduit, heavy-gauge pipe (depending on the size and weight of the particular rolled piece), or a sealed wooden dowel inserted into the cardboard tube and suspended on an appropriate support. The support device may consist of "S" hooks attached to chains bolted to the ceiling, grooved brackets on a cantilever system, or pegs made of metal or wood driven into wooden posts (fig. 19).

Fig. 19. Supports for rolled textiles: (left to right) posts, brackets, and blocks

If they cannot be suspended, covered rolled pieces can rest on shelving or in drawers, ideally with the ends of the tubes elevated with Ethafoam blocks (fig. 19) to minimize the stress on the bulkier section of the tube. Avoid stacking rolls, as this places uneven pressure on the textiles underneath.

Costume Storage

Each costume is a complex construction that deserves individual consideration before decisions are made about its storage.

> **Hanging versus Flat Storage**
>
> *If the costume is in good repair, of strong construction, and dimensionally stable, it may be a candidate for long-term vertical storage on a custom hanger.*
>
> *If the costume is beaded or heavily embellished, bias-cut, strapless, or of a very delicate or complex construction, it should be stored flat or in a large, acid-free costume storage box with acid-free tissue padding.*

Costumes that are strong enough to be hung should be supported by an *inert* hanging device that takes on the general shape of the shoulder. A molded plastic hanger or contoured wooden hanger (cut to size if necessary and sealed with a water-borne urethane coating) can be used as a framework for making padded hangers. Choose a hanger that reflects the slope of the costume's shoulder and is wide enough to support it fully. The neck of the hanger should be long enough to prevent creasing or damage to stand-up collars. Build up the shape of the shoulder and chest by wrapping the hanger with layers of polyester or cotton batting.(Polyester batting made with fibers that are bonded mechanically are considered archival; those that use an adhesive bond, sometimes evident from the slightly sticky feel, should be avoided.) Cover the padding with washed muslin and tack with a few strategically placed stitches (fig. 20).

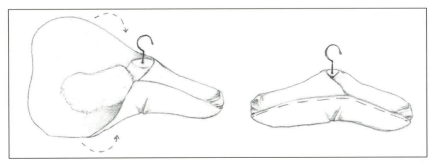

Fig. 20. Making a padded hanger

Never use uncovered wire hangers, as they rust, cause distortion and tears, and do not provide adequate support.

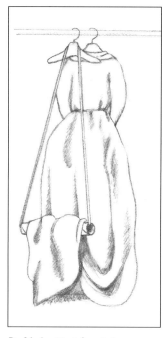

Fig. 21. A support for a train

The shoulder area should not take the total weight of heavy or elaborately shaped costumes. Trains, trousers, and long or heavy skirts should be supported by cotton twill tape stitched carefully along the waistband or seams and extending up to the hanger, thereby distributing the weight more evenly. A length of archival tube suspended from the hanger can support a train (fig. 21). Sleeves, ruffles and other fabric embellishments may also require additional support. Use soft, light-weight, acid-free tissue paper to shape these areas and thereby prevent distortions and creases from forming.

A loose-fitting muslin hanging bag for very fragile costumes or costumes with sharp or shedding components, will provide some protection for that costume as well as those adjacent to it. Costumes should not be stored in plastic bags. Some types of plastic are chemically unstable and may break down, reacting with the costume inside. Plastic, especially if sealed closed, can also trap moisture and promote mold growth.

Hang costumes so they are readily accessible and away from areas of heavy traffic. Allow adequate hanging space for each costume to avoid abrasion and creasing. A square of Tyvek suspended over the hook of the hanger, clearly marked with the costume's identification number, will simplify retrieval and minimize handling (fig. 22).

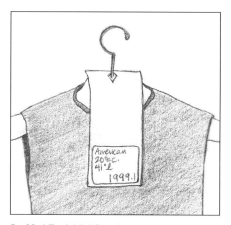

Fig. 22. A Tyvek label for a hanging costume

Housing options range from portable metal clothing racks to custom metal cabinets with adjustable hanging rods. Adequate hanging space, inert materials, dust and light protection, and air circulation are the basic requirements for any vertical storage system.

Framed or Mounted Textile Storage

Framed or mounted textiles can be a challenge to store because of their size. Ideally, a framed textile should be stored flat, allowing it to return to its natural tension. Horizontal shelving or large pull-out drawer units can meet this requirement. Unfortunately, this method of storage requires a large amount of space; therefore, other alternatives are worth considering.

Vertical storage bins constructed of metal or an acceptable wood product (see Materials for Storage and Display) will make more efficient use of the space. The frames can be inserted at an angle, face up, which will allow the textile to relax somewhat. Interleaf the frames with acid-free foamboard dividers to protect the glass and framing device. For short-term storage, framed textiles can be hung on painting racks or walls with traditional hanging hardware, such as mirror hangers and "S"-shaped hooks. ■

MOUNTING AND EXHIBITING TEXTILES

A well-designed mount allows the viewer to enjoy and understand the textile or costume on exhibit while providing it with adequate physical support. The exhibit environment is unavoidably stressful for works of art as it entails exposure to light, dust, and handling necessary for exhibit preparation (and sometimes, unfortunately, by museum visitors). A poorly designed mount or a mount made of inappropriate materials presents yet another hazard by creating undue stress on the work of art or exposing it to chemically unstable materials. No textile or costume should be on permanent display, even on a well-designed mount. Rather, a rotation schedule should be planned that will allow the works of art to rest in storage most of the time.

Mount design should begin with a careful assessment of the object and will require ingenuity and the skills necessary to fabricate the mount. Some of the most widely used mounting methods for textiles and costumes are described in general terms below. Since each work of art is different, even the most standard mounting system will have to be adjusted to meet the requirements of good mount design for that specific object. Several mounting systems should never be considered: these include the use of tacks, nails, staples, rings, adhesive tapes or non-archival adhesives to support textiles or costumes for display.

A good mount:
- *addresses any weak or vulnerable aspects of the work of art.*
- *provides adequate support.*
- *is constructed of materials that are inert and compatible with the work of art.*
- *is aesthetically pleasing.*
- *meets the interpretive objectives for display.*
- *is completely reversible.*

Textiles that are strong enough to support their own weight, such as rugs, quilts, and coverlets, can be displayed by means of a Velcro fastener or a fabric sleeve attached to the upper edge of the reverse side. A layer of muslin or polyethylene plastic sheeting should be placed behind a free-hanging textile if it is to be displayed against a wooden wall or an outside wall that might have moisture-related problems.

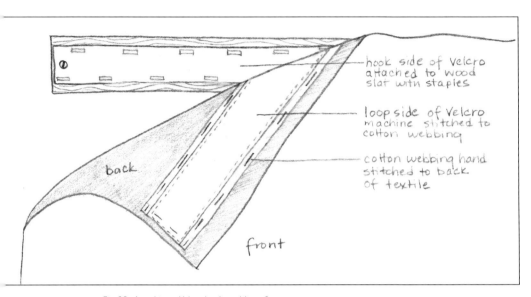

Fig. 23. Attaching a Velcro hook and loop fastener

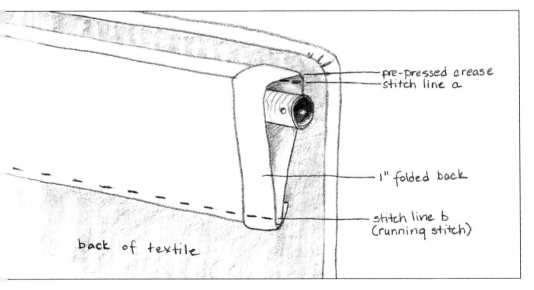

Fig. 24. Attaching a muslin sleeve

MOUNTING AND EXHIBITING TEXTILES

Velcro Fastener

The soft, or loop, side of the Velcro fastener is machine-stitched onto a length of cotton webbing (2 to 3 inches wide) or a strip of medium- to heavy-weight washed, unbleached muslin. The webbing is temporarily positioned with pins along the top of the back of the textile at least ¼ inch from the edge. Keep in mind that when the textile is hung, the fastener will be a level horizontal line on the wall and may not strictly conform to the upper edge of the textile, especially if it is irregular. The webbing is then hand-stitched onto the textile, using a running stitch with periodic backstitches (fig. 23).

It may be necessary to remove the Velcro fastener before returning the textile to storage, as it may create unequal tension in the piece when it is rolled or folded.

Fabric Sleeve

Washed, unbleached muslin that has been ironed and creased is ideal for this hanging method. The sleeve should be long enough to support the entire width of the textile and full enough to receive the hanging device, such as a dowel rod or electrical conduit. Allow for some ease to accommodate the diameter of the hanging device; otherwise, the face of the textile will be distorted when it is hanging.

Pin the sleeve fabric to the textile, positioning a prepressed crease about an inch below the textile's upper edge, in a perfectly straight horizontal line (fig. 24). The outermost edges of the fabric strip can be finished by turning the fabric under one inch at both ends. With the sleeve fabric opened out flat, sew a row of running stitches (stitch line a), spanning several threads on

> **Sewing Materials and Tools**
>
> *Use a needle that is an appropriate size for the density of the weave. Generally, a smaller needle is best (conservators often use a #12 sharp) because it will penetrate the interstices, or gaps where the threads intersect, without breaking or distorting the threads. For the same reason, the needle should penetrate the fabric at a 90° angle. Cotton is usually the thread of choice since it is fairly strong and stable, and is available in a range of colors and diameters. Cotton is neither too delicate nor too strong for most sewing jobs, whereas silk and nylon threads have poor aging properties and polyester threads are sometimes too strong for finely woven textiles. Keep a wide range of colors on hand to assure a good color match with the face of the textile.*

the face of the textile with each stitch. Next, fold the sleeve fabric to form a casing (as shown), retaining the ease for the pipe, and sew another row of running stitches (stitch line b). These stitches will penetrate all the layers of the fabric sleeve and the textile itself.

Prepare the hanging device by drilling holes ¼ inch from the ends of the hanging rod or pipe. Once the rod has been inserted into the fabric sleeve, it can be attached to the wall with nails inserted through these holes. Alternatively, a picture-hanging wire or heavy monofilament can be threaded through the pipe and attached to clips suspended from a hanging rail.

Strainers and Solid Supports

A strainer, or wooden frame, with a display fabric stretched tautly over it, is another display alternative. This mounting method is particularly well-suited to textiles that are too fragile or loosely woven to support their own weight, very distorted textiles, and textiles that require a frame or glazing material. This type of mount is made by stretching washed unbleached muslin (or a

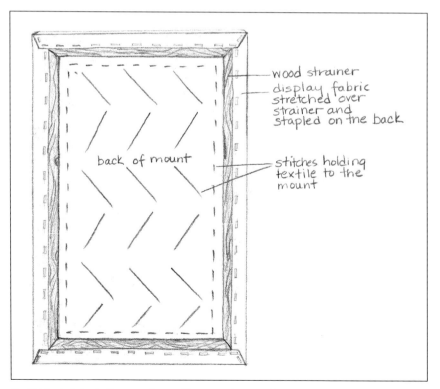

Fig. 25 Hand stitches holding a textile to a fabric-covered strainer (back view)

washfast colored cotton) over a wooden stretcher frame and securing it, under tension, on the back with rust-proof staples. (Never wrap the edges of a historical textile around a frame.) The wooden elements can be purchased at an art supply shop and easily assembled and sealed with a waterborne urethane coating to minimize offgassing. Stitch the textile to this fabric support with cotton sewing thread, keeping the needle at a 90-degree angle and passing it through all the fabric layers. Make sure the stitches span several threads on the face of the textile. Stitch along the outer dimensions of the textile and provide enough stitching in the central area to allow sufficient support for the strain of vertical hanging (fig. 25).

A solid support is a similar construction. A piece of archival mat board is recessed into the wooden frame before the display fabric is stretched over it and stapled, under tension, to the back. After the display surface is prepared, the textile is secured to the panel with a curved needle. Working with a solid support mount requires greater sewing skills because of the curved needle and should be considered only for a textile with a fairly open weave that is supple enough to accommodate this type of needle without permanently distorting or breaking the threads.

A small, light-weight textile can be mounted on a simplified version of the solid support described above. Cover a piece of heavy archival mat board with a washed cotton fabric. Secure the edges of the fabric on the back of the matboard with archival double-sided tape or an archival adhesive (see Supply Sources). Attach the textile to the display fabric with a fine curved needle.

Passive Mounts

Passive mounts are another type of mount in the display repertoire. This method is ideal when the textile cannot be stitched into, for example, a very brittle silk or a leather artifact. The textile simply rests on a platform, which is often exhibited at a slight angle, approximately 15° (fig. 26). A napped fabric, such as flannel or velvet, can be secured to the platform under the textile, providing some friction to help hold the textile in place.

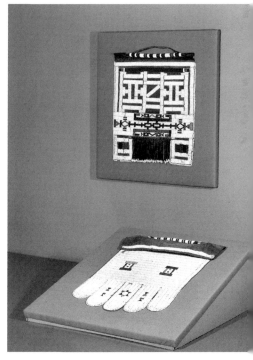

Fig. 26. A passive mount

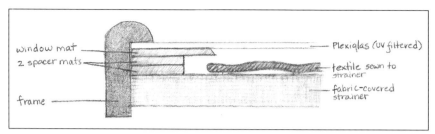

Fig. 27. Cross-section of a matted and framed textile

Matting and Framing Textiles

Matting and framing mounted textiles is not a necessary step, but can provide aesthetic enhancement and protection during display. Always use an archival-quality mat board. The window opening of the mat should be cut a little larger than the textile itself so there will be no pressure applied to the edges of the textile. Alternatively, the window mat can be elevated with a spacer so that it is suspended over the edge of the textile, but not in direct contact with it (fig. 27). If the textile is framed, the window mat itself can serve as a spacer, preventing the textile from coming into direct contact with glass or acrylic sheeting. Discuss these options with a qualified framer, preferably one associated with the Professional Picture Framers Association (PPFA) who has passed the Certified Picture Framer (CPF) exam (see Organizations).

Matted textiles that are left unframed can be covered with a layer of Mylar or acid-free tissue paper and stacked in drawers or storage boxes. They require less space than framed textiles, and storing them in this manner allows for ease of examination and handling. This type of storage mount is especially well-suited for a study or sample collection.

Fig. 28. Front view of an archival foam mount with display fabric pulled away

Pin Mounts

Another mounting method that is appropriate for some small to medium-sized textiles on short-term display is a pin mount. Similar in some respects to a solid support mount, a pin mount has an archival foam panel inside the wooden frame (fig. 28). With this method,

MOUNTING AND
EXHIBITING TEXTILES

three elements are combined to support the textile and hold it in place: The display fabric covering the mount provides some friction, entomological pins hold the textile in place, and an angled presentation minimizes the gravitational pull.

The solid support used for the pin mount is usually fabricated by screwing a 1-inch-thick Ethafoam plank into the interior of a sealed wooden frame that is larger than the textile. Keep in mind that many widely available foams are chemically unstable and, therefore, inappropriate for display purposes (see Supply Sources). The frame is then covered with a washed display fabric, ideally a fabric with some "tooth" or nap, which is secured with staples to the back of the frame. The textile is positioned on the mount and pinned into place with very fine entomological pins penetrating at a 90-degree angle. There are no hard rules about the number or spacing of the pins, but the goal is to secure the textile, especially along the top edge, without making a lot of unnecessary holes. It is helpful to diagram the placement of the pins to aid in the deinstallation of the textile, which must take place prior to storage. The mount is displayed at an angle with the lower edge held out from the wall by means of brackets or blocks. A suitable angle is created when the lower edge of the panel extends 1 to 2 inches from the wall for every 12 inches of the panel's height (see Plate 9).

Glazing Materials

Glass and acrylic sheeting, such as Plexiglas, can help protect a textile from light, dust and handling. These two materials have distinct characteristics that must be taken into account. In many applications, acrylic sheeting is the preferred material because it is light-weight and break-resistant. Some types of acrylic sheeting, such as uf-5 Plexiglas, filter ultraviolet light, thereby providing some protection for the framed textile. On the negative side, acrylic is easily scratched and has electrostatic properties, which can damage weak fibers in close contact with its surface. For these reasons, glass is often the better choice for small, severely degraded textiles, such as archeological fragments. Even then, care must be taken to allow some space between the glazing material and the textile to allow for air circulation.

Keep in mind that it is difficult and very expensive to purchase sheets of Plexiglas larger than 4 by 8 feet. Glass, too, has size constraints; even small pieces must be handled very carefully. Anything over about 36 x 48 inches would be dangerously heavy and easily broken, posing a threat to both the art handlers and the work of art.

Costume Mounts

Costume support devices are probably the most complex mounts to design and fabricate and should be carefully considered in light of both the individual costume's needs and the overall exhibit design goals.

Here are a few of the many questions that should be addressed before designing and fabricating an appropriate costume mount:

- What type of costume support will work best with the condition and construction of the costume, allowing the costume to be placed on the form and displayed with minimal stress?

- What types of undergarments, if any, are needed to support and enhance the silhouette of the costume?

- Is the exhibit emphasizing artistic/stylistic features or ethnographic features of the costumes? It may be necessary to procure mannequins that reflect the physical characteristics of the people of the culture that made the costumes.

- Will the costumes be displayed in an abstract manner (partial body forms, flat forms, etc.) or realistically with hair and defined facial features?

- Will the costumes be viewed from one angle or from all directions?

Because of their design, many costumes require a full body figure to equalize and support their total weight. Many materials can be employed to create the required form, and, once again, ingenuity is often required. Possibilities include, but are not limited to, modified department store mannequins, historical costume mannequins (see Supply Sources), and forms fabricated in-house out of carved Ethafoam disks, or wood or metal armatures covered with polyester batting (fig. 29). Two-dimensional costumes may be displayed on a t-bar or kimono stand (fig. 30). A piece of carved Ethafoam covered with muslin or soft acid-free tissue is often all that a costume accessory such as shoes or a hat will need for support. As with all mounts, use archival materials or modify non-archival materials with a physical barrier that will minimize contact with the costume.

MOUNTING AND EXHIBITING TEXTILES

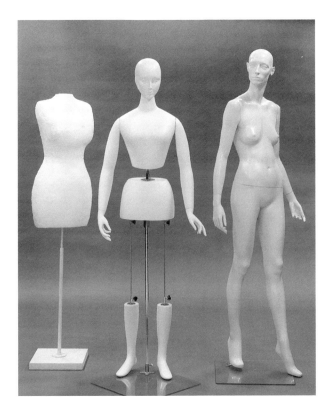

Fig. 29. (left to right) Hand-carved Ethafoam form, Wacoal period mannequin, and a department store mannequin

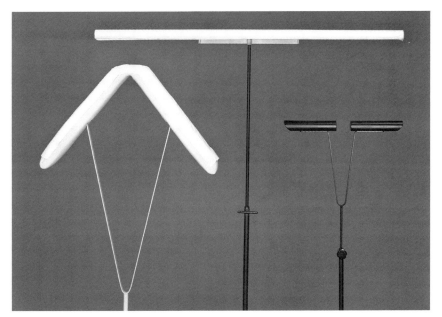

Fig. 30. Variations on the T-bar mount

Costumes of historic or artistic significance, in private and institutional collections, should never be worn for any occasion or purpose. Contemporary body shapes, undergarments and postures have changed greatly and cause too much stress on fragile garments. Perspiration, body-oil, cosmetic and fragrance stains are inevitable when a costume is worn. Although these stains may not be discernible at first, over time they will oxidize, darken and become difficult, if not impossible, to remove.

A good costume silhouette is not just a stylistic luxury but a structural necessity for three-dimensional textile objects. Period photographs and drawings can be a valuable resource, offering inspiration and information for the appropriate display of historical costumes. ■

HANDLING GUIDELINES

When handling a textile or costume, a few general rules should be observed:

- *Wash hands immediately before handling textiles. Otherwise, wear clean gloves; soiled gloves may transfer dirt.*

- *Do not smoke, eat, or drink in the exhibition, work, or storage areas. Accidents may result in stains on textiles, and food attracts insects.*

- *Use pencils for writing or sketching in the vicinity of the works of art; do not use pens, which can leave permanent marks.*

- *Before handling textiles, remove sharp jewelry that could snag or tear delicate threads.*

- *Be aware that personal items such as fresh flowers, woolen overcoats, furs and food may introduce insects into the work area.*

- *Keep light exposure to a minimum by turning off lights in galleries and work and storage areas when they are not in use.*

- *When moving a textile, place it on a rigid, flat support covered with acid-free paper, muslin, Tyvek or polyethylene plastic.*

- *Never place textiles directly on non-archival paper, cardboard or unsealed wood, as these materials may be acidic.*

- *Maintain a clean work surface by dusting or wiping the area with a clean damp cloth.*

PLATES

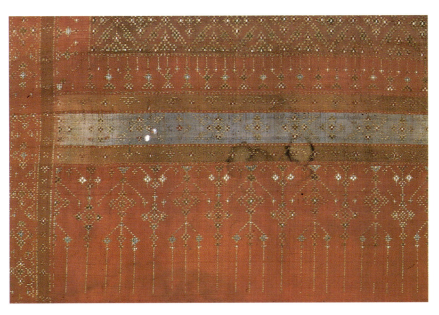

Plate 1. The incised holes in this silk textile from Thailand are evidence of insect damage. The adjacent dark rings could be water spots or the result of a spot-cleaning attempt by a previous owner. (Hip wrapper, mid-19th century, Thailand; silk and metallic threads, 127 1/2 x 37 in.; Mrs. Pierre F. Goodrich Endowed Art Fund, 1995.70.)

Plate 2. Even with the specialized equipment available in a textile conservation facility, some textiles cannot be cleaned. As the examples on these two pages illustrate, a textile's artistic and/or historical interest often makes it worthy of display despite minor imperfections. The dye in the green fabric in this quilt is extremely fugitive and would probably stain the adjacent white fabric if wet-cleaned. (Eli Lilly Family Album Quilt, 1847, Baltimore, Maryland; cotton appliquéd, pieced and embroidered, 104 1/2 x 105 in.; gift of Louise Emerson Francke, a great-great-granddaughter of Eli Lilly of Baltimore County, Maryland, 1996.281.)

Plate 3. This embroidered apron could not be safely wet-cleaned because it contains a variety of materials, including silk floss and many types of metallic thread. (Woman's apron, about 1760, Germany; silk and metallic threads, 26 x 39 in.; gift of Mr. and Mrs. W. J. Holliday, Sr., 70.46.)

Plate 4. This Baluchi prayer rug appears to be in nearly perfect condition. (Distortion caused by variations in the weave structure, as seen here, is a distinctive feature of textile art, not a flaw.) However, like many functional objects, this rug has subtle patterns of wear and some minor repairs. Such features suggest how a textile was used or valued by the people that made it, and they should be preserved, if possible. (Prayer rug, third quarter of 19th century, Baluchi people, northeastern Iran; wool, 63 x 30 in.; Colonel Jeff W. Boucher Collection, 1996.62.)

Plate 5. Art handlers at the Indianapolis Museum of Art install a Central Asian embroidery on an angled mount. This textile, like all textiles exhibited in the museum, will be on display for only a few months to protect the dyes and fibers, which are very light-sensitive. (Dowry textile or ceremonial furnishing fabric, Uzbekistan, Tashkent area, late 19th century; cotton embroidered with silk and wool threads, 104 x 90 in.; gift of Dennis R. Dodds in memory of his father, William Ray Dodds, 1997.184.)

Plate 6. This West African costume is displayed on a complex mount that provides support for all the elements while creating the illusion of movement appropriate for a dancer's costume. (Egungun masquerade costume, 20th century, Yoruba people, Nigeria; cotton cloth and glass beads, length: 61 in.; Peggy S. Gilfoy Memorial Fund, 1990.2.)

Plate 7. Couture costumes are displayed on high-fashion mannequins with minimal accessories and understated hairstyles made with nylon net, reflecting a modern aesthetic. (The Fine Art of Fashion, 1992)

Plate 8. Displayed on wall-mounted t-bars, the kimonos in this exhibition seem to float in mid-air. A low riser keeps visitors at a safe distance. (Art to Wear: Japanese Kimonos from the Collection, 1998)

Plate 9. Quilts are attached to large angled strainers with Velcro fasteners. An elastic cord running parallel to the wall serves as a discreet barrier, reminding visitors not to touch the textiles. "Do not touch" signs and security staff reinforce this important message. (Stitch by Stitch: A Quilt Potpourri, 1996)

Plate 10. This embroidered shawl is masterful in its graceful overall design as well as in the finely detailed figures and animals. The extensive deterioration (resulting from inherent vice) of the dark brown embroidery threads used to outline the figures is apparent only on close inspection. See details on cover and title page. (Shawl, late 19th century, India, Punjab; wool, silk, 68 x 70 in.; Mary Black Fund, 1995.69.)

GLOSSARY

Acidic — Measuring lower than 7 on the pH scale. The lower the number, the more acidic the substance is.

Alkaline — Measuring higher than 7 on the pH scale. The higher the number the more alkaline the substance is. The term "base" is often used to describe an alkaline substance.

Archival — This term is used to denote materials that are chemically stable and relatively permanent, desirable qualities for materials in contact with works of art.

Bias — A line diagonal to the grain of the fabric.

Buffered — A material that has had an alkaline chemical, usually calcium or magnesium carbonate, added during processing that makes it more resistant to acidification. Preferred for use with cellulose materials such as cotton and linen.

Dry-clean — To clean by immersion and agitation in an organic solvent such as perchloroethylene or stoddard solvent.

Footcandle — A unit of measurement used to describe light exposure. One footcandle is equivalent to 10 lux.

Fringe — Unwoven warp ends, often twisted or braided in a decorative manner. Fringe can also be added to the textile after weaving.

HEPA filter — A high-efficiency particulate air filter, often used with a vacuum cleaner, that is capable of removing particles larger than 0.3 micrometers from the air.

Hygrometer — An instrument used to measure relative humidity.

Inert — Chemically stable; not readily reactive.

Inherent vice — Intrinsic and irreversible instability of a material due to a chemical or process used in its manufacture.

Lux — A unit of measurement used to describe light exposure. Ten lux are equivalent to 1 footcandle.

Microclimate — A self-contained environment within a larger environmental system. A microclimate can be advantageous to a textile's preservation (for example, a display case with humidity controls) or deleterious (condensation in an enclosed space).

Mordant — A substance, usually a metallic salt, introduced during the dyeing process that increases the affinity of the dye for the fiber.

Offgassing — Emitting volatile chemicals, often acids.

pH — Refers to the concentration of hydrogen ions in a given solution. The scale ranges from 1 to 14 (from most acid to most alkaline, 7 being neutral) and can be measured, always in the presence of water, with pH strips or a pH meter.

Pheromone trap — A monitoring device that uses an insect's sex pheromones, or chemical signals, to attract male insects of that species. Such traps are useful for identification purposes and to locate areas of insect activity.

Pile — Supplementary threads that project out from the foundation weave (for example, velvets and knotted rugs).

RH (relative humidity) — The relationship between the amount of moisture present in a given volume of air and the maximum amount of moisture that could be present, expressed as a percentage.

Selvedge — The vertical edge of a textile where the wefts encircle the outermost warp threads.

Solvent — A substance that interacts with another substance (solute) to form a solution. In the context of dry cleaning, this term refers to an organic solvent, such as perchloroethylene or stoddard solvent.

Tensile strength — A fiber's capacity to resist breakage when subjected to longitudinal stress.

GLOSSARY

Unbuffered — A material that has had no alkaline chemicals added to boost its acid resistance. Preferred for contact with protein fibers, such as wool and silk.

Warp — The elements that run longitudinally through a woven fabric and that are secured to the loom prior to weaving.

Water purification — There are several ways to purify water. Each of the methods outlined below requires specialized equipment and maintenance:

> **Softened water** — A cartridge is used to remove calcium and magnesium ions. The sodium ions that remain should be eliminated in a final rinse of purer water.
>
> **Deionized water** — All ions are removed as the water runs through two cartridges.
>
> **Filtered water** — Odor, chlorine, and suspended particles of iron, silt, sand and dirt are removed from potable water by an in-line water system with various exchangeable cartridges.
>
> **Reverse osmosis** — Water is filtered through a special membrane that allows only the water, and no impurities, to pass.
>
> **Distilled water** — Water vapor from boiled water is collected and condensed, resulting in very pure water.

Water-trap vacuum — A vacuum cleaning system that employs cold tap water to trap dust and dirt.

Weft — The elements that run horizontally across a woven fabric, passing through the sheds of the loom.

Weighted silk — Certain silk fabrics that were treated with metallic salts or other additives to artificially increase their weight. Often a cause of irreversible deterioration (see **inherent vice**).

Wet-clean — To clean by immersion in water or a water-based solution.

BIBLIOGRAPHY

General Conservation

American Institute for Conservation. *Code of Ethics and Guidelines for Practice*. Washington, D.C.: American Institute for Conservation, 1994.

Bachmann, Konstanze, ed. *Conservation Concerns: A Guide for Curators and Collectors*. Washington, D.C.: Smithsonian Institution Press, 1992.

Canadian Conservation Institute. *Notes*. Ottawa: Canadian Conservation Institute, 1983.

Crafts Council. *Science for Conservators, Book 1: An Introduction to Materials; Book II: Cleaning; Book III: Adhesives and Coatings*. London: The Crafts Council, 1984.

Davis, Nancy. *Handle With Care: Preserving Your Heirlooms*. Rochester, N.Y.: Rochester Museum and Science Center, 1991.

National Committee to Save America's Cultural Collections. *Caring for Your Collection*. New York: Harry N. Abrams, 1992.

Tetreault, Jean, and Scott Williams. *Guidelines for Selecting Materials for Exhibit, Storage and Transportation*. Ottawa: Canadian Conservation Institute, 1993.

The Museum Environment

Cassar, May. *Environmental Management: Guidelines for Museums and Galleries*. London: Routledge, 1995.

Edwards, S. R., B. M. Bell, and M. E. King, eds. *Pest Control in Museums: A Status Report*. Lawrence, Kansas: Association of Systematics Collections, 1981.

Illuminating Engineering Society of North America. *Museum and Art Gallery Lighting: A Recommended Practice*. New York: Illuminating Engineering Society of North America, 1996.

Kay, Gersil N. *Fiber Optics in Architectural Lighting: Systems, Design, and Applications.* New York: McGraw-Hill Companies, 1999.

Pinniger, David. *Insect Pests in Museums.* London: Archetype, 1994.

Pinniger, David, and Peter Winsor. *Integrated Pest Management: Practical, safe and cost-effective advice on the prevention and control of pests in museums.* London: Museums and Gallery Commission, 1998.

Strang, Thomas J. K. "A Review of Published Temperatures for the Control of Pest Insects in Museums." *Collection Forum* 8, no. 2 (1992): 41-67.

Thomson, G. *The Museum Environment.* London: Butterworth & Co., 1978.

Textile and Costume Conservation

The Conservation of Tapestries and Embroideries. Proceedings of Meetings at the Institut Royal du Patrimoine Artistique, Brussels, Belgium, September 21-24, 1987. Marina del Rey, California: The Getty Conservation Institute, 1987.

Flury-Lemberg, Mechthild. *Textile Conservation and Research.* Bern: Schriften der Abegg-Stiftung, 1988.

Landi, Shiela. *The Textile Conservator's Manual,* 2nd ed., Oxford: Butterworth, 1992.

Mailand, Harold F. *Considerations for the Care of Textiles and Costumes: A Handbook for the Non-Specialist.* Indianapolis: Indianapolis Museum of Art, 1980.

McLean, Catherine C., and Patricia Connell. *Textile Conservation Symposium in Honor of Pat Reeves.* Los Angeles: The Conservation Center, Los Angeles County Museum of Art, 1986.

Thurman, Christa Mayer C. *The Department of Textiles at the Art Institute of Chicago.* Chicago: The Art Institute, 1989.

Textile Techniques and Terminology

Burnham, D. K. *Warp and Weft, a Textile Terminology.* Toronto: Royal Ontario Museum, 1980.

Emery, Irene. *The Primary Structure of Fabrics.* Washington, D.C.: The Textile Museum, 1980.

Gilfoy, Peggy Stoltz. *Fabrics in Celebration from the Collection.* Indianapolis: Indianapolis Museum of Art, 1983.

Mallett, Marla. *Woven Structures: A Guide to Oriental Rug and Textile Analysis.* Atlanta: Christopher Publications, 1998.

Seiler-Baldinger, Annemarie. *Textiles: A Classification of Techniques.* Washington, D.C.: Smithsonian Institution Press, 1994.

The Textile Institute. *Identification of Textile Materials.* 7th ed. Manchester, England: The Textile Institute, 1975.

APPENDIX A: MATERIALS FOR STORAGE AND DISPLAY

Materials that are considered safe:

Adhesives — Certain acrylics and polyvinyl acetate solutions, which should be individually tested. Includes some adhesive tapes such as 3M #415, which is not to be used in direct contact with textiles.

Fabrics — Cotton, linen or silk that is pre-washed (colorfast), desized. Virgin polyester without adhesives.

Foams — Polyethylene (Ethafoam, Volara), polystyrene.

Plastics — Polyethylene, polypropylene, Tyvek.

Physical barriers — Barrier film (aluminized Mylar or Marvaseal), polyester film (Mylar), medium- to heavy-weight acid-free paper or board, polyethylene plastic sheeting.

Sealants — Air-drying lacquer, acrylic latex paint, water-based urethanes, two-part epoxy coatings. Important: Sealants must be completely cured prior to exposure to works of art.

Wood — Low-acid varieties such as poplar, walnut, spruce, mahogany, birch and balsa that have been properly sealed.

Wood products — Those that contain phenol formaldehyde adhesive: Type 1, type AA, or type BB (exterior grade) plywood, and Medex fiberboard that have been properly sealed.

APPENDIX B: SUPPLY SOURCES

The companies below offer some of the materials and equipment mentioned in this handbook; their inclusion does not constitute an endorsement nor should this list be considered comprehensive. The authors and the Indianapolis Museum of Art cannot be held responsible for the quality or use of these products.

Acrylic sheeting (UV filtering) — vitrine and mount fabrication

Museum Acrylics Co.
216 Ashwood Ln. N.W.
New Philadelphia, OH 44663
(330) 308-5411
FAX (330) 308-5411

See "UV filtering materials," pg. 84, for additional sources.

Art supplies

Many local art supply stores carry a selection of useful tools and materials, including Krylon 1303 crystal clear acrylic resin spray coating (for identification labels) and stretcher bars. These items can also be ordered through mail order sources such as:

Pearl Paint Company
308 Canal St.
New York, NY 10013
(800) 451-7327
FAX (800) 732-7591
FAX (212) 431-5420
www.pearlpaint.com

Sax Arts and Crafts
P.O. Box 510710
New Berlin, WI 53151
(800) 558-6696
FAX (800) 328-4729
www.saxarts.com

Conservation supplies — general

These companies carry a range of supplies for textile care, including tools, detergents, pH pens, and notions:

Gaylord Bros.
P.O. Box 4901
Syracuse, NY 13221-4901
(800) 448-6160
FAX (800) 272-3412
www.gaylord.com

Talas
568 Broadway
Suite 107
New York, NY 10012
(212) 219-0770
FAX (212) 219-0735
www.talas-nyc.com

University Products, Inc.
517 Main St.
P.O. Box 101
Holyoke, MA 01041-0101
(800) 628-1912
FAX (800) 532-9281
www.universityproducts.com

Cotton twill tape

Testfabrics
415 Delaware Ave.
P.O. Box 26
West Pittston, PA 18643
(570) 603-0432
FAX (570) 603-0433
www.testfabrics.com

Ely Yawitz
1717 Olive St.
P.O. Box 14325
St. Louis, MO 63178-4325
(800) 325-7915
FAX (314) 231-3820

Entomological pins

Carolina Biological Supply
2700 York Rd.
Burlington, NC 27215
(800) 334-5551
FAX (800) 222-7112
www.carolina.com

Ethafoam (220 polyethylene foam plank and 221 foam sheet)

Republic Packaging
9160 S. Green St.
Chicago, IL 60620
(773) 233-6530
FAX (773) 233-6005
www.repco.com

Preservation Products
178 West Boden St.
Milwaukee, WI 53207
(800) 448-6070
FAX (800) 322-6525

Fabrics

Baer Fabrics
515 E. Market St.
Louisville, KY 40202
(800) 769-7776
FAX (502) 582-2331

Thai Silks
252 State St.
Los Altos, CA 94022
(650) 948-8611
FAX (650) 948-3426
www.thaisilks.com

Fabrics — undyed, desized

Testfabrics
415 Delaware Ave.
P.O. Box 26
West Pittston, PA 18643
(570) 603-0432
FAX (570) 603-0433
www.testfabrics.com

Hangers — molded plastic

Henry Hanger Co.
450 Seventh Ave.
New York, NY 10123
(212) 279-0852
FAX (212) 594-7302

**Laboratory supplies
(glassware, pH test strips)**

Fisher Scientific
711 Forbes Ave.
Pittsburgh, PA 15219-4785
(800) 766-7000
FAX (800) 926-1166
www.fishersci.com

Mannequins

Dorfman Museum Figures
840 Oella Ave.
Ellicott City, MD 21043
(800) 634-4873
FAX (410) 750-7987

Stockman Forms
Pucci International Ltd.
44 West 18th St.
New York, NY 10011
(212) 633-0452
FAX (212) 633-1058

Wacoal Corp.
7, shichijo goshonouchi
 nakamachi shimogyou-ku
Kyoto, 600-8862 Japan
(075) 321-8011
FAX (075) 321-9219

**Monitoring equipment —
hygrometers, pH meters**

ACR Systems, Inc.
Herzog/Wheeler + Associates
2183 Summit Ave.
St. Paul, MN 55105
(651) 647-1035
FAX (651) 647-1041

Cole-Palmer Instrument Company
625 East Bunker Ct.
Vernon Hills, IL 60061-1844
(847) 549-7600
FAX (847) 247-2929

Fisher Scientific
711 Forbes Ave.
Pittsburgh, PA 15219-4785
(800) 766-7000
FAX (800) 926-1166
www.fishersci.com

**Needles —
surgical (curved)**

Talas
568 Broadway
Suite 107
New York, NY 10012
(212) 219-0770
FAX (212) 219-0735

Hospital Marketing Services
Industrial Park
P.O. Box 1217
Naugatuck, CT 06770
(800) 786-5094
FAX (203) 723-7248
www.hmsmedical.com

**Paper products —
archival quality**

The following companies carry a wide selection of archival paper products, boxes, rolling tubes, etc.:

Archivart
7 Caesar Pl.
Moonachie, NJ 07074
(800) 804-8428
FAX (201) 935-5964
www.archivart.com

APPENDIX B

Conservation Resources,
International, L.L.C.
8000-H Forbes Pl.
Springfield, VA 22151
(800) 634-6932
FAX (703) 321-0629

Gaylord Bros.
P.O. Box 4901
Syracuse, NY 13221-4901
(800) 448-6160
FAX (800) 272-3412
www.gaylord.com

Hollinger Corporation
P.O. Box 8360
Fredericksburg, VA 22404
(800) 634-0491
FAX (800) 947-8814

Light Impressions Corporation
439 Monroe Ave.
P.O. Box 940
Rochester, NY 14603-0940
(800) 828-6216
FAX (800) 828-5539
www.lightimpressionsdirect.com

University Products, Inc.
517 Main St.
P.O. Box 101
Holyoke, MA 01040-0101
(800) 628-1912
FAX (800) 532-9281
www.universityproducts.com

Pheromone traps (species specific)

Insects Limited, Inc.
16950 Westfield Park Rd.
Westfield, IN 46074
(317) 896-9300
FAX (317) 867-5757
www.insectslimited.com

Polyethylene plastic film

Most hardware stores

Steamers

Jiffy Steamer Company
P.O. Box 869
Union City, TN 38261-0869
(901) 885-6690
FAX (901) 885-6692
www.jiffysteamer.com

Storage units — metal

Delta Designs
P.O. Box 1733
Topeka, KS 66601
(800) 656-7426
FAX (785) 233-1021
www.deltaltd.com

Montel, Inc.
1333 Gateway Dr.
Suite 1009
Melbourne, FL 32901
(800) 772-7562
(407) 726-9777
www.montel.com

Spacesaver Corporation
1450 Janesville Ave.
Fort Atkinson, WI 53538
(800) 862-5036
www.spacesaver.com

Tyvek

Masterpak
50 W. 57th St.
New York, NY 10019
(800) 922-5522
FAX (212) 586-6961
www.masterpak-usa.com

UV filtering materials — acrylic sheeting, tube sheaths, film

Solar Screen
5311 105th St.
Corona, NY 11368
(718) 592-8222
FAX (888) 271-0891
www.solar-screen.com

Talas
568 Broadway
Suite 107
New York, NY 10012
(212) 219-0770
FAX (212) 219-0735
www.talas-nyc.com

University Products, Inc.
517 Main St.
P.O. Box 101
Holyoke, MA 01040-0101
(800) 628-1912
FAX (800) 532-9281
www.universityproducts.com

Vacuum cleaners with HEPA filters

Museum Services Corp.
1107 E. Cliff Rd.
Burnsville, MN 55337-1514
(800) 672-1107
FAX (612) 895-5298

Nilfisk of America
300 Technology Dr.
Malvern, PA 19355
(800) 645-3475
FAX (610) 647-6427
www.pa.nilfisk-advance.com

Lab Safety Supply Inc.
P.O. Box 1368
Janesville, WI 53547-1368
(800) 356-0783
FAX (800) 543-9910
www.labsafety.com

Vacuum cleaners — micro-attachments

Clotilde
B 3000
Louisiana, MO 63353
(800) 772-2891
FAX (800) 863-3191
www.clotilde.com

Vacuum cleaners — water-trap vacuum

Rainbow Cleaning Systems
Rexair, Inc.
3221 W. Big Beaver Rd., Suite 200
Troy, MI 48084
(248) 643-7222
FAX (248) 643-7676
www.RainbowSystem.com

APPENDIX C: ORGANIZATIONS

The American Institute
for Conservation (AIC)
and FAIC Guide to
Conservation Services
1717 K St., N.W.
Suite 301
Washington, D.C. 20006
(202) 452-9545
FAX (202) 452-9328
www.palimpsest.stanford.edu/aic

Canadian Conservation
Institute (CCI)
1030 Innes Rd.
Ottawa, Ontario,
Canada K1A 0M5
(613) 998-3721
FAX (613) 998-4721
www.pch.gc.ca/cci-icc

The Costume Society of
America (CSA)
55 Edgewater Dr.
P.O. Box 73
Earleville, MD 21919
(800) CSA-9447
FAX (410) 275-8936
www.costumesocietyamerica.com

International Fabricare
Institute (IFI)
Textile Analysis Laboratory
12251 Tech Rd.
Silver Spring, MD 20904
(800) 638-2627
FAX (301) 236-6320
www.ifi.org

International Institute for
Conservation of Historic
and Artistic Works (IIC)
6 Buckingham St.
London, England WC2N 6BA UK
44 (0) 171 839 5975
FAX 44 (0) 171 976 1544

Professional Picture Framers
Association (PPFA)
4305 Sarellen Rd.
Richmond, VA 23231-4311
(800) 556-6228
FAX (804) 222-2175
www.ppfa.com

Other Internet Resources

Conservation on-line
http://palimpsest.stanford.edu/

Indianapolis Museum of Art
www.ima-art.org

Smithsonian Institution
www.si.edu

The Textile Museum
www.textilemuseum.org

Gallery labels and printed handouts remind museum visitors not to touch the works of art:

WHY WE ASK YOU NOT TO TOUCH

We hope your grandchildren—and their grandchildren—will someday visit our museum.

We hope the works of art you are enjoying will be here for them to see in the future, in the same fine condition.

Which is why we ask you not to touch.

Textiles are among the most fragile of all museum objects, and damage to textiles in museums is often caused by visitors. The familiarity and tactile qualities of quilts and other textiles may tempt visitors to touch and handle them, but such touching shortens considerably the life of these precious reminders of our cultural heritage.

Please help us preserve our museum's collection.

INDEX

Note: Page references to plates and illustrations are indicated in italics.

A

acidic, defined, 71
acrylic sheeting
    as glazing material, *52, 53*
    sources of, 80, 84
adhesives
    damaging, 37, 47
    recommended, 79
air circulation, 20
alkaline, defined, 71
American Institute for Conservation of Historic and Artistic Works (AIC), 15
anionic detergent, 31
Anthrenus verbasci (carpet beetles), 24–27
archival, defined, 71
archival materials for storage and display, 37–38
    paper and boxes, 38
    sources of, 82–83
aromatic deterrents for insects, 25
art supplies, sources of, 80

B

beetles. *See* carpet beetles
bias, *15*
    defined, 71
blocking, 33
boxes, archival, 38
    sources of, 82–83
brushes for surface cleaning, 29
buffered, defined, 71

C

cardboard tubes for rolled storage, 41
    sources of, 82-83
carpet beetles *(Anthrenus verbasci)*, 24–27
cellulose materials, 38
chiffon, 35
cleaning, 29–35
    dry, 34–35
    spot, 34
    surface, 29–30
    wet, 30–34
climate control, 19–20
    air circulation and, 20
clothes moths *(Tineola bisselliella)*, 24–27
colorfast dyes, 31
conservation, 13
    preservation and, 14
    preventative care and, 14
    as profession, 13–15
    restoration and, 14
    reversibility of, 14
    supplies for, 80–81
conservator
    training, 14
    locating a, 15
costumes
    display of, *66, 67, 68*
    folding, 40
    handling guidelines, 57
    hanging, 44
    labels for, 44
    mounting, 54–56
    storage for, 43–45
    twill tape supports for, 44
    wearing of, 56
cotton thread, 49
cotton twill tape, sources of, 81
crepe, 35
custodianship, 15–18

D

damaged areas
    from light, 21
    treatment of, 35–36
deionized water, 31
    defined, 73
distilled water, 31
    defined, 73
documentation, 15–18
dry cleaning, 34–35
    defined, 71
dry-cleaning bags, 35
dryers, automatic, 32
dyes, colorfast, 31

E

edges, stabilizing, 35–36
entomological pins
    for pin mounting, 53
    source of, 81
environment, 19–27
    climate control and, 19–20
    insects and rodents in, 24–26
    lighting and, 21–23
    mold and, 23–24
    tools for monitoring, *20*
Ethafoam
    for mounts, 53
    source of, 81
    storage supports, *42, 43*
exhibitions
    costume, *66, 67, 68*
    textile, *65, 69*

F
fabrics, new, for support or display
    recommended, 79
    source of, 81
fiber-optic lighting, 22
filtered water, defined, 73
filters, air, 20
filters, for ultraviolet light, 21
    sources of, 80, 84
flat storage, 39, 40
    versus hanging storage, 43
fluorescent lights, 21
foam mounts, 52–53
foams, recommended, 79
footcandles, 22
    defined, 71
framed textiles, 52
    storage, 39, 45
freezing procedure for textiles, 26
fringe, *15*, 41
    defined, 71
fringe folder, 42
fumigation for insects, 27
fungi, 23

G
glass, as glazing material, for protecting textiles, 53
glazing materials, 53
gloves, cotton, 57
Guide to Conservation Services (AIC), 15

H
halogen lighting, 22
handling guidelines, textiles and costumes, 57
hangers
    padded, 43
    source of, 81
hanging bag, muslin, 44
hanging storage, 43–45
    versus flat storage, 43
health problems and mold, 24
HEPA (high efficiency particulate air) filter, 24
    defined, 71
high-twist fabrics, 35
humidification, 35
humidity, 19
    mold and, 23
    tools for monitoring, 19–20
hygrometers, 19, *20*
    defined, 71
    sources of, 82

I
incandescent lights, 22
inert, defined, 71
inherent vice, 16, *70*
    defined, 71
insects, 24–26
    aromatic deterrents for, 25
    carpet beetles *(Anthrenus verbasci)*, 25
    clothes moths *(Tineola bisselliella)*, 25–26
    damage, caused by, 26, *61*
    freezing, to control, 26, 27
    fumigation for, 27
integrated pest management (IPM), 24
Internet resources, 85
iron mordant, 16
ironing, 33

L
labels
    for textiles, 18
    for costumes, 44
laboratory supplies, sources for, 82
light, 21–23
    calculating exposure, 22
    damaging effect of, 21
    types of, 21–22
light-sensitive materials, rotation schedule for, 23
lux, 22
    defined, 72

M
mannequins, 54–55
    sources of, 82
materials for storage and display
    archival, 37–38
    recommended, 79
    sources of, 80–84
matting textiles, 52
metallic threads or elements, 40
microclimate, defined, 72
mildew, 23
mold 23-24
    health problems and, 24
monitoring equipment, sources of, 82
mordant, 16
    defined, 72
mothballs, 25
moths. See clothes moth
mount design, 47
mounting and exhibiting textiles, 47–56
    costume mounts, 54–56
    glazing materials, 53
    matting and framing, 52
    muslin sleeves, *48*, 49–50

INDEX

passive mounts, 51
pin mounts, 52–53
sewing materials and tools, 49
strainers and solid supports, 50–51
Velcro fasteners, *48*, 49
multilayered textiles, rolling, 42

N
natural fibers, climate control and, 19
needles, 49, 51
surgical, sources of, 82
nylon net to stabilize damaged areas, 36

O
offgassing, 37
defined, 72
organizations, 85
Orvus WA Paste (sodium lauryl sulfate), 31

P
padded hangers, making, 43
paper products-archival quality, 37–38
sources of, 82–83
paradichlorobenzene, 25
passive mounts, 51
pest managers, professional, 27
pH
archival materials and, 38
defined, 72
of paper products, 37
of textiles, 29
of water, measuring, 33
pH meters, sources of, 82
pH pen, 37
pH scale, *38*
pheromone traps, 24
defined, 72
source of, 83
physical barriers, recommended, 79
pile, defined, 72
pile fabrics, rolled storage for, 41
pin mounts, 52–53
pins for mounting, 53
source of, 81
plastic sheeting, 37
plastics, recommended, 79
poison bait for rodents, 27
polyethylene plastic film, 37
source of, 83
preservation, 14
preventative care, 14
profession, textile conservation as, 13–15
professional conservators, 14–15
protein fibers, 38

R
relative humidity (RH), 19
defined, 72
restoration, 14
reverse osmosis, defined, 73
reversibility of conservation, 14
RH (relative humidity), 19,
defined, 72
rodents, 24–26
prevention, 27
rolled storage, 39, 41–43
cardboard tubes for, 41
multilayered textiles, 42
for pile fabrics, 41
supports for, 42–43
rotation schedule for light-sensitive materials, 23

S
screens, vacuuming through, 30
sealants, 38, 43, 51, 53
recommended, 79
selvedges, *15*, 41,
defined, 72
silks, weighted, 16, *17*
defined, 73
silverfish, 26
sleeve, for hanging, *48*, 49–50
sodium lauryl sulfate, 31
softened water, defined, 73
solvents
cleaning with, 34–35
defined, 72
spiders, 27
spot cleaning, 34
stabilizing damaged areas, 35–36
stains, 29, 34
steamers, source of, 83
sticky traps for insects, 24, 26
storage, 37–45
archival materials for, 37–38
costume, *40*, 43–45
flat, 40
framed or mounted textile, 45
metal units, sources of, 83–84
rolled, 41–43
strainers, mounting, 50–51
sunlight, damaging effect of, 21
as mold inhibitor, 23–24
supply sources, 80–84
supports
for display, 50–53
for rolled textiles, 42–43
surface cleaning, 29–30

T
T-bar mounts for costumes, 54–55
tensile strength, 19
    defined, 72
tests to detect harmful components of materials, 37
textile handling guidelines, 57
Tineola bisselliella (clothes moths), 24–27
tissue paper
    acid-free, 38, 40
    non-archival, 35, 37
trains, support for, 44
Tyvek, for storage, 40, 41, 42, 44, 79
    source of, 84
Tyvek costume labels, 44

U
ultraviolet light, 21, 22
    filtering materials, sources of, 84
unbuffered materials, 38
    defined, 73

V
vacuum cleaners, 29
    sources of, 84
vacuuming, 29–30
Velcro fasteners, 47, 48–49, 69

W
warp *15*, 41
    defined, 73
washers, automatic, 32
washing. *See* wet cleaning
water-based stains, 34
water for cleaning, 31–32
water purification methods, defined, 73
water-trap vacuums, 24,
    defined, 73
wearing costumes, 56
weft, *15*
    defined, 73
weighted silks, 16, *17*
    defined, 73
wet cleaning, 30–34
    chamber, 32
    defined, 73
    guidelines, 31
    for mold, 24
    risks associated with, 14, 29–31, 34
    support during, 32
wood and wood products
    problems with, 37
    recommended, 79
    sealing, 38